The Folger Shakespeare Filmography
Written and Edited By
Barry M. Parker

Folger Books
Published by the Folger Shakespeare Library
Department of Museum and Public Programs

The Folger Library is Administered by
The Trustees of Amherst College
O. B. Hardison, Jr., Director

This Filmography made possible in part
through financial assistance provided by
The National Endowment for the Humanities
and The Rockefeller Foundation

The Folger Shakespeare Filmography

The Folger Shakespeare Filmography was produced in part through financial assistance provided by The National Endowment for the Humanities (Grant Number 27-606-77-1363) and The Rockefeller Foundation.

Patti Pancoe, Editorial Assistant

Film stills from the Museum of Modern Art and The American Film Institute.

Book design by Tom Jones and Jane Firor Kearns.

Library of Congress Card Catalog Number 79-3141

I.S.B.N. 0-918016-19-3

Copyright 1979 by The Folger Shakespeare Library.

No part of this book may be reproduced in any form without permission in writing from the publisher, except a reviewer who wishes to quote brief passages or entries in connection with a review written for inclusion in newspapers, magazines, or scholarly works.

Manufactured in The United States of America.

CONTENTS

	Page
Foreword	5
Introduction	7
Feature Length Versions of the Plays of Shakespeare	11
Feature Length Adaptations or Derivatives of Shakespearean Plays	25
Dance, Musical, or Operatic Versions of the Plays	41
Educational, Instructional, and Abridged Versions of the Plays	47
Appendix One: Incidentals	53
Appendix Two: Additional Listings of Films Representing Shakespeare	55
Suggested Readings	59
Index	61

Cover photo: *Romeo and Juliet,* 1936

Foreword

In 1975, after years of planning, the Folger Library established a study collection of Shakespeare and Shakespeare adaptations on film. The rapid growth of this study collection during the ensuing years was greatly assisted by grants from the Rockefeller Foundation of New York and the National Endowment for the Humanities.

Although the Folger film collection consists solely of composite safety prints, all material is stored according to International Federation of Film Archive (FIAF) regulations. The collection has been used continually by scholars, researchers, and educators since it was established. This filmography is a natural outgrowth of these activities.

The work of Mr. Joseph G. Empsucha was central in establishing efficient procedures for cataloging, storage, film use, and bibliographical control. Much of the work in this filmography reflects the excellent job which he did. Mr. Barry Parker carried forward Mr. Empsucha's work with great energy and creative insight. It is hoped that the present volume will be useful to the growing number of teachers, scholars, librarians, and others who are involved in this important and fascinating area of Shakespeare studies.

O. B. Hardison, Jr.
Director
Folger Shakespeare Library

A Midsummer Night's Dream, 1935

Introduction

If history is ever rewritten, and great literature along with it, Mark Antony may well disappear and be replaced by the person of Marlon Brando. Such has been the effect on so many of us from viewing Joseph L. Mankiewicz's 1953 film production of *Julius Caesar*. Brando *was* Mark Antony, as James Mason was a tortured Brutus and Louis Calhern a dignified Caesar. The Mankiewicz film is easily the most well-known of any motion picture version of Shakespeare's works. Seemingly endless numbers of high school students were granted dispensation to cut classes and embark on a great expedition to see the film, college actors were forever imitating Brando, and the commercial success of the film has forever been a delight to M-G-M. Surprisingly, however, Mankiewicz's film was not the first sound version of Caesar; a graduate school student named David Bradley earned that honor in 1950 using a cast made up largely of Northwestern University students. A young Charlton Heston played Mark Antony, a role he improved upon when he once again performed as Antony twenty years later in Stuart Burge's film of *Julius Caesar*. The 1970 *Caesar* clearly showed that the new freedom of the cinema had affected Shakespeare as well. Touches of nudity, implied homosexuality, and the very bloody death of Caesar (in color) were included in the film. The M-G-M backlots had been replaced by location shooting in Spain, and hundreds of extras that had never heard of the Screen Actors Guild were cast as the countrymen of Rome.

"Julius Caesar" is not the only work of Shakespeare to be adapted for film on more than one occasion. The major purpose of this filmography, therefore, is to shed as much light as possible on the numerous Shakespearean motion pictures produced over the past five decades. In all, this catalog has data on five versions of "Hamlet," three of "Macbeth," three of "Othello," four of "Romeo and Juliet," and three filmings of "A Midsummer Night's Dream," among many others.

There is often controversy surrounding filmmaking based on works of the great writers, and films adapted from Shakespeare have proven no exception. Orson Welles, himself the director of three film journeys into Shakespeare, once remarked that he ". . . was doubtful about Shakespeare for the movies; for while (they) do most everything better than the stage, they don't do verse better." Welles was not alone in his feelings about the movies and Shakespeare. For decades, critics and scholars have debated whether filmmakers had any business bastardizing what they considered to be a pure theater art. Films based on Shakespeare's plays seldom follow the text faithfully; in many cases characters have been eliminated (or new ones made up), dialogue has been rewritten or cut, and entire scenes placed in a different order. Furthermore, directors and producers often wish their product to bear a stamp of individuality; therefore many Shakespearean films carry unique interpretations that stray from the classical approach.

Whatever the criticisms of Shakespearean cinema may be, it has not deterred director after director who sought to take on the often awesome task of perfecting Shakespeare on film. Nor has this phenomenon been limited geographically. Films of Shakespeare's works are truly universal; the United States, the Soviet Union, Britain, Japan, Germany, Spain, Czechoslovakia, and France have all been countries of origin for the numerous films mentioned.

The listings for this filmography begin with the first feature-length Shakespearean sound picture, the 1929 *The Taming of the Shrew*. I have excluded silent features for two reasons: one, the subject was extensively covered in Robert Hamilton Ball's excellent book, *Shakespeare on Silent Film;* and two, the majority of the early silent Shakespearean features or shorts are not easily available for rental. The British Film Institute, The Library of Congress, and The Folger Shakespeare Library all have extensive silent material in their collections, but these films are for study purposes only; also many of these films are incomplete and may prove unsuitable for general audience study.

For purposes of clarity and to avoid duplication of titles or misinterpretations of genres, this filmography has been divided into four sections: (1) feature length versions of the plays of Shakespeare; (2) feature length adaptations or derivatives of Shakespearean plays; (3) dance, musical, or operatic versions of the plays; (4) educational, instructional, and abridged versions of the plays. Hopefully, this will eliminate the possibility of films from the same play source (e.g. "Romeo and Juliet") being confused with another film that may have the same title. In films where the use of Shakespeare's writings or characters was minimal, or the films themselves were unusual, appendices have been added to mention these features, as well as to give some basic information about them.

I have kept most of my comments and notes about these films to a minimum. This filmography is not intended to be a critique or literary analysis; therefore, comments about a particular film are included only to provide additional information about a title. In most cases, I have included these comments in the adaptations and dance/opera sections only.

For the most part, I have not included television productions in these listings. Shakespeare on television is a subject worthy of filling a separate catalog; furthermore, the majority of these productions were never intended for theatrical release, and were recorded on either video tape or originally done "live" with only kinescope records of them remaining. Therefore, they are not classified as *films* for the purposes of this filmography. In cases where a film was intended for both television broadcast and theatrical release (George Schaefer's *Macbeth* or Olivier's *Richard III* are two examples) they have been included. This is not meant to slight such fine television productions as Joseph Papp's *Much Ado About Nothing,* the Laurence Olivier *Merchant of Venice,* or the current BBC Shakespeare series.

Certain foreign pictures, which were believed never to have been shown theatrically in the United States, or whose general distribution was kept to such a minimum as to make them virtually unknown, have not been included. Details about these films are spotty at best, and in some cases, non-existent.

The majority of the films mentioned in this listing are available for rental or lease in 16mm format, that being the gauge most commonly used in classroom or instructional situations today. Ownership and distribution of films frequently change however, and the studio of original release mentioned with a specific title should not automatically be assumed to be the current distributor. Many of these films are available for modest rentals, especially if an admission fee is not charged. Also, some distributors have made their entire collections available on video tape, with long term lease and/or purchases possible. For more information on rental or lease of motion pictures, I refer you to: James L. Limbacher's *Feature Films on 8mm, 16mm, and Video Tape* (R.R. Bowker Company) and *Film Programmer's Guide to 16mm Rentals* by Linda J. Artel and Kathleen Weaver, published by the San Francisco Community Press.

It is inevitable in preparing a listing such as this one that omissions and factual errors may occur. Sources of information used in preparing this filmography were often conflicting, and I have attempted to eliminate any possible error by checking and re-checking every conceivable source. These would include various film periodicals, newspaper and magazine reviews, legal files of the motion picture companies that produced the films, catalogs of companies releasing the films, pressbooks and publicity material relating to a film, and as often as possible, the film itself. In particular, the following sources of information were invaluable: *American Film Institute Catalogs 1921-30* and *1961-70; The British Film Catalog: 1895-1970; Catalog of Copyright Entries for Motion Pictures;* Copyright Office of the Library of Congress; *Daily Variety; Film and Literature Quarterly; Film Daily; Films in Review; Film News; The Filmgoers Companion; Films and Filming; The Films of Orson Welles; Guide to Dance on Film; Guide to Television and Radio; Hollywood Reporter; Learning Corporation of America Film Listings; Motion Pictures, Television and Radio: A Union Catalog; The New Film Index; The New York Times Film Reviews; Shakespeare on Film Newsletter; Sight and Sound; T.V. Movies, Feature Films on 8mm, 16mm and Video Tape; Variety; Who Was Who on Screen.*

I would like to express my appreciation to the following individuals who provided information, assistance, and encouragement: Michael Clark, Chris Spilsbury, Debbie Davidson, and Paul Page of The American Film Institute in Washington; Anne Schlosser of The American Film Institute West in Los Angeles; David Parker, Madeline Matz, Emily Sieger, and in particular Barbara Humphries, from The Library of Congress Motion Picture Section; Ron Magliozzi, Mary Rosenfeld, and Bob Summers from The Museum of Modern Art Department of Film; Mary Corliss of The Museum of Modern Art Film Stills Archive; Robert Rosen and Robert Gitt of The U.C.L.A. Film Archive; Audree Malkin of The U.C.L.A. Theater Arts Library; Judith Schwartz and Mary Ahern of The Museum of Broadcasting; Kenneth Rothwell of the *Shakespeare On Film Newsletter;* and Judy Jarodnick of R.R. Bowker Company.

I would also like to thank Burton Shapiro for his advice and assistance; Charlton Heston for his interest and encouragement; Jane Kearns and Tom Jones for countless hours of advice on the preparation of this filmography; and especially Gail Levine, Film Librarian for Queens College (SUNY) who provided me with much of her time and technical assistance in preparing this work.

Furthermore, my great thanks to the staff of The Folger Shakespeare Library, especially the staff of Public Programs: Leni Spencer, supervisor, Janet Alexander, JoAnn Azzarello, JoAnn Feldman, Velma Edwards, Liam Rector, and Bob Eisenstein, all of whom gave me their support during the more difficult times of this project.

—Barry M. Parker, July 1979

The Taming of the Shrew, 1967

Feature Length Versions

Each of the following films is based on a particular work of Shakespeare.

Antony and Cleopatra

Great Britain/Spain. 1973. 160 minutes. Folio Films, London and Izaro Films, Madrid. Technicolor. 35mm. Todd-AO 35. Stereophonic sound.
Producer: Peter Snell. **Director and Screen Adaptation:** Charlton Heston. **Photographer:** Rafael Pacheco. **Production Designer:** Maurice Pelling. **Art Directors:** Jose Alguero (exteriors), Jose MaAlarcon (interiors). **Editor:** Eric Boyd-Perkins. **Music:** John Scott and Augusto Algero. **Sound:** George Stephenson.
Cast: Charlton Heston (Antony); Hildegard Neil (Cleopatra); Eric Porter (Enobarbus); John Castle (Octavius); Fernando Rey (Lepidus); Juan Luis Gallardo (Alexas); Carmen Sevilla (Octavia); Freddie Jones (Pompey); Alba (Schoolmaster); Peter Arne (Menas); Warren Clarke (Scarus); Roger Delgado (Soothsayer); Julian Glover (Proculeius); Sancho Gracia (Canidius); Garrick Hagon (Eros); John Hallam (Thidias); Jane LaPortaire (Charmian); Joe Melia (The Messenger); Monica Peterson (Iras); Emiliano Redondo (Mardian); Aldo Sambrel (Ventidius); Felipe Solano (Soldier); Douglas Wilmer (Agrippa).
Note: Filmed on location in Almeria and Madrid, Spain.

As You Like It

Great Britain. 1936. 98 minutes. Twentieth Century-Fox Film Corporation. Black and white. 35mm.
Producer and Director: Paul Czinner. **Screenplay:** Robert J. Cullen. **Photographer:** Hal Rosson. **Music:** William Walton, played by the London Philharmonic Orchestra.
Cast: Elisabeth Bergner (Rosalind); Laurence Olivier (Orlando); Henry Ainley (Banished Duke); Sophie Stewart (Celia); Mackenzie Ward (Touchstone); Leon Quartermaine (Jaques); Richard Ainley (Silvius); Felix Aylmer (Duke Frederick); Aubrey Mather (Corin); Fisher White (Adam); George Moore Marriott (Dennis); John Laurie (Oliver); Lionel Braham (Charles); Austin Trevor (Le Beau); Cavin Gordon (Amiens); Cyril Horrocks (First Lord); Ellis Irving (Second Lord); Lawrence Hanray (Third Lord); Joan White (Phebe); Dorice Fordred (Audrey); Peter Bull (William).

Hamlet

Great Britain. 1948. 153 minutes. Two Cities Films, released by J. Arthur Rank Organisation. Black and white. 35mm.
Producer and Director: Laurence Olivier. **Photographer:** Desmond Dickenson. **Art Director:** Carmen Dillon. **Editor:** Helga Cranston. **Music:** William Walton, played by the Philharmonia Orchestra, conducted by Muir Mathieson and John Hollingsworth. **Sound:** John W. Mitchell and Harry Miller.

Cast: Laurence Olivier (Hamlet); Eileen Herlie (The Queen); Basil Sydney (The King); Jean Simmons (Ophelia); Felix Aylmer (Polonius); Norman Wooland (Horatio); Terence Morgan (Laertes); Harcourt Williams (First Player); Patrick Troughton (Player King); Tony Tarver (Player Queen); Peter Cushing (Osric); Stanley Holloway (Gravedigger); Russell Thorndyke (Priest); John Laurie (Francisco); Esmond Knight (Bernardo); Anthony Quayle (Marcellus); Niall MacGinnis (Sea Captain).
Note: Voted Best Picture of the Year in 1948 by The Motion Picture Academy of Arts and Sciences. Olivier also won an Academy Award for Best Actor for his performance as Hamlet.

Hamlet

USA. 1964. 186 minutes. Electronovision Productions, American Broadcasting, Paramount Theatres, Inc., Theatro-film; distributed by Warner Brothers Pictures. Black and white. 35mm (Electronovision).
Producers: William Sargent, Jr., Alfred W. Crown, John Heyman. **Executive Producer:** Alexander H. Cohen. **Electronovision Director:** Bill Colleran. **Staged by:** John Gielgud. **Video:** Carl Hanseman. **Editor:** Bruce Pierce. **Sound:** James Fitch.
Cast: Michael Ebert (Francisco); Barnard Hughes (Marcellus); Robert Milli (Horatio); Alfred Drake (Claudius); Philip Coolidge (Voltimand); John Cullum (Laertes); Hume Cronyn (Polonius); Richard Burton (Hamlet); Eileen Herlie (Gertrude); Linda Marsh (Ophelia); John Gielgud (Ghost); Dillon Evans (Reynaldo); Clement Fowler (Rosencrantz); William Redfield (Guildenstern); George Voskovec (Player King); Geoff Garland (Lucianus); George Rose (First Gravedigger).
Note: Filmed June 30 and July 1, 1964 during the regular performances of the play which opened in New York April 9, 1964.

Hamlet

(Gamlet)
USSR. 1964. 148 minutes. Lenfilm, released by Lopert Pictures. Black and white. 35mm. Sovscope.
Director: Grigoriy Kozintzev. **Screenplay:** Grigoriy Kozintzev, from the Russian language translation by Boris Pasternak. **Photographer:** A. Chechulin. **Art Director:** Yevgeniy Yeney and G. Kropachyov. **Editor:** Ye. Makhankova. **Music:** Dmitriy Shostakovic, played by Leningrad Philharmonic Orchestra, conducted by N. Rabinovich. **Sound:** B. Khutoryanskiy.
Cast: Innokenti Smoktunovsky (Hamlet); Mikhail Nazvanov (King); Elsa Radzin (Queen); Yuri Tolubeyev (Polonius); Anastasia Vertinskaya (Ophelia); Vladimir Erenberg (Horatio); Stepan Oleksenko (Laertes); Vadim Medvedev (Guildenstern); I. Dmitriyev (Rosencrantz); A. Krevalid (Fortinbras); V. Chekoerski (Gravedigger).
Note: In Russian, with English subtitles. Filmed on location along the Estonian seacoast.

Hamlet

Federal Republic of Germany (West Germany). 1960. 130 minutes. Bavaria Atelier GmbH Production, released by Emerson Film Enterprises. Black and white. 35mm.
Producer: Hans Gottschalk. **Director and Screen Adaptation:** Franz Peter Wirth. **Photographers:** Kurt Gewissen, Hermann Gruber, Rudolf H. Jakob, Boris Geriup. **Music:** Rolf Unkel. **English Dubbing Director:** Edward Dmytryk.
Cast: Maximilian Schell (Hamlet); Hans Caninberg (Claudius); Wanda Rotha (Gertrude); Dunja

Movar (Ophelia); Franz Schafheitlin (Polonius); Dieter Kirchlechner (Laertes); Karl Michael Vogler (Horatio); Eckard Dux (Rosencrantz); Herbert Botticher (Guildenstern); Karl Lieffen (Osric); Rolf Boysen (Bernardo); Michael Paryla (Francisco); Alexander Engel (The Ghost); Adolf Gershing (First Player); Paul Verhoeven (Gravedigger).
Note: This West German film version was originally made for television presentation on Eurovision. Its U.S. theatrical release was in 1968, running time 120 minutes, dubbed in English.

Hamlet

Great Britain. 1970. 118 minutes. Woodfall Films-Filmways Ltd., released by Columbia Pictures. Technicolor. 35mm. MPAA Rating G.
Producer: Neil Hartley. **Executive Producers:** Leslie Linder and Martin Ransohoff. **Director:** Tony Richardson. **Photographer:** Gerry Fisher. **Design:** Jocelyn Herbert. **Editor:** Charles Rees. **Music:** Patrick Gowers. **Sound Editor:** Don Deacon.
Cast: Nicol Williamson (Hamlet); Anthony Hopkins (Claudius); Judy Parfitt (Gertrude); Mark Dignam (Polonius); Marianne Faithfull (Ophelia); Michael Pennington (Laertes); Gordon Jackson (Horatio); Ben Aris (Rosencrantz); Clive Graham (Guildenstern); Peter Gale (Osric).
Note: U.S. release of this film in 1969, running time 114 minutes.

Henry V

Great Britain. 1944. 137 minutes. A Two Cities Film, released by United Artists. Technicolor. 35mm.
Producer and Director: Laurence Olivier. **Screenplay:** Alan Dent and Laurence Olivier. **Photographer:** Robert Krasker. **Art Director:** Paul Sheriff. **Editor:** Reginald Beck. **Music:** William Walton, played by the London Symphony, conducted by Muir Mathieson. **Sound:** John Dennis and Desmond Dew.
Cast: Laurence Olivier (King Henry V); Robert Newton (Ancient Pistol); Leslie Banks (Chorus); Renee Asherson (Princess Katharine); Esmond Knight (Fluellen): Leo Genn (The Constable of France); Felix Aylmer (Archbishop of Canterbury); Ralph Truman (Mountjoy, the French Herald); Harcourt Williams (King Charles VI of France); Ivy St. Helier (Alice, Lady-in-Waiting); Ernest Thesiger (Duke of Beri); Max Adrian (The Dauphin); Frances Lister (Duke of Orleans); Valentine Dyall (Duke of Burgundy); Russell Thorndike (Duke of Bourbon); Michael Shepley (Captain Gower); Morland Graham (Sir Thomas Erpingham); Gerald Case (Earl of Westmoreland): Janet Burnell (Queen Isabel of France); Nicholas Hannen (Duke of Exeter); Robert Helpmann (Bishop of Ely); Freda Jackson (Mistress Quickly); Jimmy Hanley (Williams); John Laurie (Captain Jamie); Niall MacGinnis (Captain MacMorris); George Robey (Sir John Falstaff); Roy Emerton (Lieutenant Bardolph); Griffith Jones (Earl of Salisbury); Arthur Hambling (Bates); Frederick Cooper (Corporal Nym); Michael Warre (Duke of Gloucester).

Julius Caesar

USA. 1950. 90 minutes. Avon Productions. Black and white. 16mm.
Producer and Director: David Bradley. **Photographer:** Louis McMahon. **Music:** John Becker, played by members of the Chicago Symphony Orchestra, conducted by Grant Fletcher. **Sound:** Art Foy.
Cast: Harold Tasker (Julius Caesar); David Bradley (Brutus); Grosvenor Glenn (Cassius); Charlton Heston (Mark Antony); Helen Ross (Calpurnia); Molly Darr (Portia); William Russell (Casca).

Note: Using a budget of about $15,000, David Bradley shot this version of *Julius Caesar* in and around Chicago. Using Northwestern University student actors, and ingenious methods of cutting costs, Bradley created a curious but nevertheless interesting film. Due to great interest surrounding the film at various festivals, the film was picked up for theatrical release by Brandon Pictures; both Bradley and Charlton Heston were signed shortly thereafter to Hollywood contracts.

Julius Caesar

USA. 1953. 120 minutes. Metro-Goldwyn-Mayer. Black and white. 35mm. Stereophonic sound.
Producer: John Houseman. **Director:** Joseph Mankiewicz. **Photographer:** Joseph Ruttenberg. **Art Directors:** Cedrick Gibbons and Edward Carfagno. **Editor:** John Dunning. **Music:** Miklos Rozsa. **Sound:** Douglas Shearer.
Cast: Louis Calhern (Julius Caesar); Marlon Brando (Mark Antony); James Mason (Brutus); John Gielgud (Cassius); Edmond O'Brien (Casca); Greer Garson (Calpurnia); Deborah Kerr (Portia); George Macready (Marullus); Michael Pate (Flavius); Richard Hale (A Soothsayer); Alan Napier (Cicero); John Hoyt (Decius Brutus); Tom Powers (Metellus Cimber); William Cottrell (Cinna); Jack Raine (Trebonius); Ian Wolfe (Ligarius); Morgan Farley (Artimidorius); Bill Phipps (Servant to Antony).

Julius Caesar

Great Britain. 1970. 117 minutes. Commonwealth United Productions, released by American International Pictures. Technicolor. 35mm. Panavision. MPAA Rating G.
Producer: Peter Snell. **Executive Producers:** Henry T. Weinstein and Anthony B. Unger. **Director:** Stuart Burge. **Screen Adaptation:** Robert Furnival. **Photographer:** Ken Higgins. **Art Director:** Maurice Pelling. **Editor:** Eric Boyd-Perkins. **Music:** Michael J. Lewis. **Sound:** Paddy Cunningham.
Cast: Charlton Heston (Mark Antony); Jason Robards (Brutus); John Gielgud (Julius Caesar); Richard Johnson (Cassius); Robert Vaughn (Casca); Richard Chamberlain (Octavius Caesar); Diana Rigg (Portia); Jill Bennett (Calpurnia); Christopher Lee (Artemidorus); Alan Browning (Marullus); Norman Bowler (Titinius); Andrew Crawford (Volumnius); David Dodimead (Lepidus); Peter Eyre (Cinna the Poet); Edwin Finn (Publius); Derel Godfrey (Decius Brutus); Michael Gough (Metellus Cimber); Paul Hardwick (Messala); Thomas Heathcote (Flavius).
Note: Location scenes filmed in Spain.

King Lear

Great Britain/Denmark. 1970. 137 minutes. Filmways, Inc. in association with the Royal Shakespeare Company, released by Columbia Pictures. Black and white. 35mm.
Producer: Michael Birkett. **Director and Screenplay:** Peter Brook. **Photographer:** Henry Kristiansen. **Editor:** Kasper Schyberg.
Cast: Paul Scofield (King Lear); Irene Worth (Goneril); Jack MacGowran (Fool); Alan Webb (Duke of Gloucester); Cyril Cusack (Duke of Albany); Patrick Magee (Duke of Cornwall); Robert Lloyd (Edgar); Tom Fleming (Earl of Kent); Susan Engel (Regan); Annelise Gabold (Cordelia); Ian Hogg (Edmund); Barry Stanton (Oswald); Soren Elung Jensen (Duke of Burgundy).

King Lear
(Korol' Lir)

USSR. 1970. 136 minutes. A Lenfilm Production, released in the U.S. by Artkino Pictures, Inc. Black and white. 35mm. Sovscope.
Director: Grigoriy Kozintsev. **Screen Adaptation:** Grigoriy Kozintsev from the translation by Boris Pasternak. **Photographer:** Jonas Gricius. **Music:** Dmitriy Shostakovic.
Cast: Yuri Jarver (King Lear); Elsa Radzins (Goneril); Galina Volchek (Regan); Valentina Shendrikova (Cordelia); Ofar Dal (Fool); Kiril Sebris (Earl of Gloucester); Leonid Merzin (Edgar); Regimanias Adomaitis (Edmond); Victor Emelvanov (Earl of Kent).
Note: Film is in Russian language with English subtitles.

Macbeth

USA. 1946. 80 minutes. A Willow Production. Black and white. 16mm.
Producer: David Bradley. **Director:** Thomas A. Blair. **Screenwriter, Photographer, Editor:** David Bradley.
Cast: David Bradley (Macbeth); Jain Wilimovsky, William Bartholomay, J. Royal Mills, Louis Northrop, Ralph Beebe.
Note: David Bradley, then a student at Northwestern University, was able to raise $5,000 to produce this feature length *Macbeth*. Using college actors, Northwestern campus buildings, and a scavenger's eye for other location work (stone quarries, churches, etc.), Bradley's film was quite professional, and avoided the clumsiness that usually accompanies an amateur production. Working with Bradley (as costume designer) on this project was Charlton Heston; the two men would later work together on the 1950 *Julius Caesar,* directed by Bradley and starring Heston as Mark Antony (see page 14).

Macbeth

U.S.A. 1948. 105 minutes. A Mercury Production, released by Republic Pictures. Black and white. 35mm.
Producer, Director and Screenplay: Orson Welles. **Photographer:** John L. Russell and William Bradford. **Art Director:** Fred Ritter. **Editor:** Louis Lindsay. **Music:** Jacques Ibert, conducted by Efrem Kurtz. **Sound:** John Stransky, Jr. and Garry Harris.
Cast: Orson Welles (Macbeth); Jeanette Nolan (Lady Macbeth); Dan O'Herlihy (Macduff); Roddy McDowell (Malcolm); Edgar Barrier (Banquo); Alan Napier (A Holy Father); Erskine Sanford (Duncan); John Dierkes (Ross); Keene Curtis (Lennox); Peggy Webber (Lady Macduff); Lionel Braham (Siward); Archie Heugly (Young Siward); Jerry Farber (Fleance); Christopher Welles (Macduff Child); Morgan Farley (Doctor); Lurene Tuttle (Gentlewoman); Brainerd Duffield (First Murderer); William Alland (Second Murderer); George Chirelio (Seyton); Brainerd Duffield, Lurene Tuttle, Peggy Webber (The Three Witches).
Note: The history of Welles' *Macbeth* has left much confusion over its actual running time. Originally released in 1948 at a length believed to be 105 minutes, the film was withdrawn from circulation shortly thereafter due to the inaudibility of a bizarre pre-recorded Scottish-British soundtrack. The film was subsequently re-released in 1949 and 1950, with a re-recorded and re-mixed sound track, and a shortened running time. 16mm prints of *Macbeth* in circulation today are generally believed to be 86 minutes, although it is possible some may be as long as 95 minutes. The mystery of the running time of Welles' original version (hopefully) may be solved soon, as the UCLA Film Archive has discovered most of Welles' original cut in the vaults of

National Telefilm Associates. NTA acquired most of Republic Studio's productions after Republic went out of business.

Macbeth

United States/Great Britain. 1960. 80 minutes. Grand Prize Films, released by Prominent Films. Technicolor. 35mm.
Producer: Phil C. Samuels. **Executive Producer:** Sidney Kaufman. **Director:** George Schaefer. **Screen Adaptation:** George Schaefer and Anthony Squire. **Photographer:** F.A. Young. **Art Director:** Edward Carrick. **Editor:** Ralph Kemplen. **Music:** Richard Addinsell, played by Sinfonia of London, conducted by Muir Mathieson.
Cast: Maurice Evans (Macbeth); Judith Anderson (Lady Macbeth); Michael Hordern (Banquo); Ian Bannen (Macduff); Felix Aylmer (Doctor); Malcolm Keen (Duncan); Megs Jenkins (Gentlewoman); Jeremy Brett (Malcolm); Barry Warren (Donalbain); William Hutt (Ross); Charles Carson (Caithness); Trader Faulkner (Seyton).
Note: Filmed on location in Scotland. The first U.S. presentation was an 80 minute version on NBC Television's "Hallmark Hall of Fame" in 1960. Subsequent U.S. theatrical release was in 1963, running time—107 minutes.

Macbeth

Great Britain. 1971. 140 minutes. Playboy Productions/Caliban Films, released by Columbia Pictures. Technicolor. 35mm. Todd-AO 35. MPAA Rating R.
Producer: Andrew Braunsberg. **Director:** Roman Polanski. **Screenplay:** Roman Polanski and Kenneth Tynan. **Photographer:** Gil Taylor. **Editor:** Alastair McIntyre. **Music:** The Third Ear Band. **Choreographer:** Sally Gilpin.
Cast: Jon Finch (Macbeth); Francesca Annis (Lady Macbeth); Martin Shaw (Banquo); Nicholas Selby (Duncan); John Stride (Ross); Stephan Chase (Malcolm); Paul Shelley (Donalbain); Terence Bayler (Macduff); Andrew Laurence (Lennox); Frank Wylie (Mentieth); Bernard Archard (Angus); Bruce Purchase (Caithness); Keith Chegwin (Fleanca); Noel Davis (Seyton); Noelle Rimmington (Young Witch); Maisia MacFarquhar (Blind Witch); Elsie Taylor (First Witch).

A Midsummer Night's Dream

USA. 1935. 132 minutes. Warner Brothers. Black and white. 35mm.
Producer: Max Reinhardt. **Directors:** Max Reinhardt and William Dieterle. **Screen Adaptation:** Charles Kenyon and Mary C. McCall, Jr. **Photographer:** Hal Mohr, with special photographic effects by Fred Jackman, Byron Haskin, H.F. Koenekamp. **Editor:** Ralph Dawson. **Music:** Felix Mendelssohn, with musical arrangement by Erich Wolfgang Korngold. **Dance Director:** Nijinska.
Cast: James Cagney (Bottom); Joe E. Brown (Flute); Hugh Herbert (Snout); Frank McHugh (Quince); Victor Jory (Oberon); Olivia de Havilland (Hermia); Ross Alexander (Demetrius); Grant Mitchell (Egeus); Nini Theilade (First Fairy); Verree Teasdale (Hippolyta); Dick Powell (Lysander); Jean Muir (Helena); Ian Hunter (Theseus); Anita Louise (Titania); Mickey Rooney (Puck); Dewey Robinson (Snug); Hobart Cavanaugh (Philostrate); Otis Harian (Starveling); Arthur Treacher (Ninny's Tomb); Billy Barty (Mustard Seed).

A Midsummer Night's Dream
(Sen Noci Svatojanske)

Czechoslovakia. 1959. 80 minutes. Ceskoslovensky Film, released by Showcorporation. Eastman color. 35mm. CinemaScope.
Producer, Director and Screenwriter: Jiri Trnka. **Director of English Adaptation:** Howard Sackler. **Animators:** Jan Karpas, Stanislav Latal, Vlasta Jurajdova, Bretislav Pojar, Jan Adam, Bohumil Sramek. **Photographer:** Jiri Vojta. **Art Director:** Jiri Trnka. **Editor:** Hana Walachova. **Music:** Vaclav Trojan. **Sound:** Emanuel Formanek, Josef Vleck, Emil Polednik. **English Version Dialogue Supervisor:** Len Appelson.
Cast: Richard Burton (Narrator); Tom Criddle (Lysander); Ann Bell (Hermia); Michael Meacham (Demetrius); John Warner (Egeus); Barbara Leigh-Hunt (Helena); Hugh Manning (Theseus); Joss Ackland (Quince); Alec McCowen (Bottom); Stephen Moore (Flute); Barbara Jefford (Titania); Jack Guillim (Oberon); Roger Shepherd (Puck); Laura Graham (Hippolyta).
Note: This puppet film had no dialogue in the original Czech version. It was re-released in 1961 with an English sound track, running time—74 minutes.

A Midsummer Night's Dream

Great Britain. 1968. 124 minutes. A Royal Shakespeare/Filmways Production. Eastman Color. 35mm.
Director: Peter Hall. **Photographer:** Peter Suschitzky. **Designer:** John Bury. **Editor:** Jack Harris. **Music:** Guy Woolfenden.
Cast: Derek Godfrey (Theseus); Barbara Jefford (Hippolyta); Ian Holm (Puck); Paul Rogers (Bottom); Sebastian Shaw (Quince); Diana Rigg (Helena); David Warner (Lysander); Judi Dench (Titania); Clive Swift (Snug); Ian Richardson (Oberon); Michael Jayson (Demetrius); Bill Travers (Snout).
Note: Originally produced for theatrical release in Great Britain in 1968, this film was presented on American television (CBS) on February 9, 1969.

Othello

USA. 1952. 91 minutes. Mercury Productions, released by United Artists. Black and white. 35mm.
Producer and Director: Orson Welles. **Photographers:** Anchise Brizzi, G. Araldo, George Fanto. **Editors:** Jean Sachs, with Renzo Luoidi and John Shepridge. **Music:** Francesco Lavagnino, Alberto Barberis, conducted by Willi Ferrero.
Cast: Orson Welles (Othello); Michael MacLiammoir (Iago); Suzanne Cloutier (Desdemona); Robert Coote (Roderigo); Milton Edwards (Brabantio); Michael Lawrence (Cassio); Fay Compton (Emilia); Nicholas Bruce (Ludovico); Jean Davis (Montano); Doris Dowling (Bianca).
Note: The actual production of *Othello* took place over a four year period (1948-1952) with principal photography in Morocco (Mogador) and Venice. Despite a rather unorthodox shooting and editing schedule, *Othello* was awarded The Grand Prix at the 1952 Cannes Film Festival. For additional information on the story of Welles' film, I suggest you read *Put Money In Thy Purse,* by Michael MacLiammoir, Methuen Press, London (1952).

Othello
(Otello)
USSR. 1956. 108 minutes. A Mosfilm Production, released in the U.S. by Universal-International. Sovcolor. 35mm.
Director: Sergei Yutkevich. **Scenario:** Sergei Yutkevich; adaptation by Boris Pasternak and Anna Radlow. **Photographer:** Evgeny Andrikanis. **Art Directors:** A. Vaisfeld, V. Dorrer, M. Karyakin, O. Kroutchinia, N. Tchikirev, and A. Alexandrovskaia. **Editor:** K. Aleyeva. **Music:** Aram Khachaturian. **Sound:** B. Volsky.
Cast: Sergei Bondarchuk (Othello); Andrei Popov (Iago); Irina Skobtseva (Desdemona); Vladimir Soshalsky (Cassio); E. Vesnik (Roderigo); A. Maximova (Emilia); E. Teterin (Brabantio); M. Troyinovsky (Duke of Venice); A. Kelbeter (Montano); N. Brilling (Ludovico); L. Ashrafova (Bianca).
Cast (English voices): Howard Marion Crawford (Othello); Arnold Diamond (Iago); Katherine Byron (Desdemona); Patrick Westwood (Cassio): Richard Warner (Roderigo); Nancy Nevinson (Emilia); Michael Moore (Brabantio); Oliver Burt (Doge); Roger Snowdon (Ludovico); Ybanne Churchman (Bianca).
Note: This film was part of a United States-Soviet Union cultural exchange program; it was dubbed in English. English version in Technicolor, directed by William de Lane Lea.

Othello
Great Britain. 1965. 166 minutes. B.H.E. Productions, released by Warner Brothers Pictures. Technicolor. 35mm. Panavision.
Producers: Anthony Havelock-Allan and John Brabourne. **Director:** Stuart Burge. **Stage Director for National Theatre of Great Britain:** John Dexter. **Photographer:** Geoffrey Unsworth. **Film Art Director:** William Kellner. **Editor:** Richard Marden. **Music:** Richard Hampton.
Cast: Laurence Olivier (Othello); Frank Finlay (Iago); Maggie Smith (Desdemona); Robert Lang (Roderigo); Anthony Nicholls (Brabantio); Derek Jacobi (Cassio); Harry Lomax (Duke of Venice); Terence Knapp (Duke's officer); Joyce Redman (Emilia); Stella Reid (Bianca); Roy Holder (Clown); Michael Turner (Grafiano); Kenneth Mackintosh (Lodovico); Edward Hardwicke (Montano).
Note: This is a film version of the National Theatre of Great Britain stage production, which opened in London April 21, 1964. London opening of the film—1966.

Richard III
Great Britain. 1956. 155 minutes. Presented by Laurence Olivier in association with London Films, released by Lopert Films Distributing Corporation. Technicolor. 35mm. VistaVision.
Producer and Director: Laurence Olivier. **Photographer:** Otto Heller. **Art Director:** Carmen Dillon. **Editor:** Helga Cranston. **Music:** William Walton.
Cast: Laurence Olivier (Richard III); Ralph Richardson (Buckingham); John Gielgud (Clarence); Claire Bloom (Lady Anne); Cedric Hardwicke (King Edward IV); Alex Clunes (Hastings); Pamela Brown (Jane Shore); Mary Kerridge (Queen Elizabeth); Norman Wooland (Catesby); Helen Hayes (Duchess of York—Queen Mother); George Woodbridge (Lord Mayor of London); John Phillips (Norfolk).
Note: This film premiered simultaneously in movie theaters and on the NBC Television network nationwide.

Romeo and Juliet

U.S.A. 1936. 126 minutes. Metro-Goldwyn-Mayer. Black and white. 35mm.
Producer: Irving Thalberg. **Director:** George Cukor. **Screen Adaptation:** Talbot Jennings.
Photographer: William Daniels. **Art Director:** Cedric Gibbons. **Editor:** Margaret Booth.
Music: Herbert Stothart. **Dance Director:** Agnes deMille.
Cast: Norma Shearer (Juliet); Leslie Howard (Romeo); John Barrymore (Mercutio); Edna May Oliver (Nurse); Basil Rathbone (Tybalt); C. Aubrey Smith (Lord Capulet); Andy Devine (Peter); Ralph Forbes (Paris); Reginald Denny (Benvolio); Maurice Murphy (Balthasar); Conway Tearle (Prince of Verona); Henry Kolker (Friar Laurence); Robert Warwick (Lord Montague); Virginia Hammond (Lady Montague); Violet Kemble Cooper (Lady Capulet).

Romeo and Juliet

Great Britain. 1954. 142 minutes. A J. Arthur Rank Organisation presentation, released by United Artists. Technicolor. 35mm
Producers: Sandro Ghenzi in association with Joseph Janni. **Director and Screen Adaptation:** Renato Castellani. **Photographer:** Robert Krasker. **Editor:** Sydney Hayers. **Music:** Roman Vlad, conducted by Lambert Williamson. **Sound:** John E. Dennis and Gordon K. McCallum. **Sound Editors:** Harry Miller and Winston Ryder.
Cast: Laurence Harvey (Romeo); Susan Shentall (Juliet); Flora Robson (The Nurse); Mervyn Johns (Friar Laurence); Bill Travers (Benvolio); Enzo Flermonte (Tybalt); Aldo Zollo (Mercutio); Giovanni Rota (Prince of Verona); Sebastian Cabot (Capulet); Lydia Sherwood (Lady Capulet); Norman Wooland (Paris); Gullio Garbinetti (Montague); Nietta Zocchi (Lady Montague); Dagmar Josipovich (Rosaline); Luciano Bodi (Abraham); Thomas Nicholls (Friar John); John Gielgud (Chorus).
Note: Most of the film was shot on location in Venice, Verona, Siena and various well-preserved medieval towns.

Romeo and Juliet

Italy/Spain. 1964. 90 minutes. Imprecine-Hispamer Films, released in the U.S. by World Entertainment Corp. Eastman Color. 35mm. CinemaScope.
Director and Screen Adaptation: Ricardo Freda. **Photographer:** Gabor Pogany. **Art Director:** Teddy Villalba. **Editors:** Anna Amidei and Antonio Gimeno. **Music:** Petr Ilich Tchaikovsky and Sergei Rachmaninoff, arranged by Bruno Nicolai. **Spanish Version Music:** Jose Pagan and Antonio Ramirez Angel. **Sound:** Giovanni Rossi. **English Dubbing Director:** George Higgins III.
Cast: Gerald Meymer (Romeo); Rosemarie Dexter (Juliet); Carlos Estrada (Mercutio); Umberto Raho (Friar Laurence); Toni Soler (Nurse); Andrea Bosic (Capulet); Antolella Della Porta (Lady Capulet); Jose Marco Davo (Paris); German Grech (Tybalt); Mario DeSimone (Peter); Bruno Sciponi (Balthasar); Franco Balducci (Benvolio); Elsa Vazzoler (Lady Montague); Antonio Gradoli (Montague).
Note: The film was shot on location in Rome, Verona, Avila, and Madrid. It was released in Italy in 1964 as *Giulietta e Romeo;* in Spain as *Los Amantes de Verona;* running time—95 minutes.

Romeo and Juliet

Great Britain/Italy. 1968. 139 minutes. B.H.E. Productions, Verona Productions, Dino DeLaurentiis Cinematografica, released by Paramount Pictures. Technicolor. 35mm.

Producer: Anthony Havelock-Allan and John Brabourne. **Director:** Franco Zeffirelli. **Screenplay:** Franco Brusatti, Franco Zeffirelli, Masolino D'Amico. **Photographer:** Pasquale DeSantis. **Art Director:** Luciano Puccini and Emilio Carcona. **Editor:** Reginald Mills. **Music:** Nino Rota.
Cast: Leonard Whiting (Romeo); Olivia Hussey (Juliet); Milo O'Shea (Friar Laurence); Michael York (Tybalt); John McEnery (Mercutio); Pat Herwood (The Nurse); Natasha Perry (Lady Capulet); Robert Stephens (Prince of Verona); Bruce Robinson (Benvolio); Laurence Olivier (Narrator).
Note: The film was shot on location in Tuscany, including Pienza in Tuscania, Artena, Gubbio, and at the Borghese Palace. It was released in London in 1968 as *Romeo e Giulietta;* original running time—152 minutes.

The Taming of the Shrew
U.S.A. 1929. 63 minutes. United Artists. Black and white. 35mm.
Director and Screen Adaptation: Sam Taylor. **Photographer:** Karl Struss. **Art Directors:** William Cameron Menzies and Laurence Irving. **Editor:** Alien McNeil. **Sound:** David Forrest. **Titles and Opticals:** Consolidated Film Industries.
Cast: Douglas Fairbanks (Petruchio); Mary Pickford (Katherine); Edwin Maxwell (Baptista); Joseph Cawthorn (Gremio); Clyde Cook (Grumio); Geoffrey Wardwell (Hortensio); Dorothy Jordan (Bianca).
Note: For the 1966 reissue of this film, a re-recorded sound track with a new musical score and sound effects were added. For this version, release was by Cinema Classics; producer: Matty Kemp; editor: John F. Link.

The Taming of the Shrew
(La bisbetica domata)
U.S.A./Italy. 1967. 122 minutes. Royal Films International, F.A.I.; released by Columbia Pictures. Technicolor. 35mm. Panavision.
Producers: Elizabeth Taylor, Richard Burton, Franco Zeffirelli. **Executive Producer:** Richard McWhorter. **Director:** Franco Zeffirelli. **Screenplay:** Paul Dehn, Suso Cecchi D'Amico, Franco Zeffirelli. **Photographer:** Oswald Morris. **Art Directors:** Elven Webb and Giuseppe Mariani. **Editor:** Peter Taylor. **Music:** Nino Rota, conducted by Carlo Savina. **Sound:** Aldo DeMartini and Mario Ottani. **Dubbing Editors:** Graham Harris and Janet Davidson.
Cast: Elizabeth Taylor (Katharina); Richard Burton (Petruchio); Cyril Cusack (Grumio); Michael Hordern (Baptista); Alfred Lynch (Tranio); Alab Webb (Gremio); Giancarlo Cobelli (The Priest); Natasha Pyne (Bianca); Michael York (Lucentio); Victor Spinetti (Hortensia); Roy Holder (Biondello); Mark Dignam (Vincentio); Bice Valori (The Widow); Gianni Magni (Curtis); Lino Capolicchio (Gregory); Roberto Antonelli (Philip); Alberto Bonucci (Nathaniel).

Twelfth Night or What You Will
(Dvenadtsataia Noch)
USSR. 1955. 88 minutes. A Lenfilm Production. Agfacolor. 35mm.
Director and Screenplay: Yan Fried. **Photographer:** E. Shapiro. **Art Director:** S. Malkin. **Music:** A. Zhivotov.
Cast: Katya Luchko (Viola/Sebastian); Anna Larianova (Olivia); V. Medvediev (Duke Orsino); M. Yanshin (Sir Toby Belch); G. Vipin (Sir Andrew Azuecheek); V. Merkuriev (Mavolio); S.

Lukyanov (Antonio); B. Friendlich (Clown); A. Lisyanskaya (Maria); S. Flippov (Fabian); A. Antonov (Sea Captain).
Note: This film is in the Russian language; English subtitles.

Romeo and Juliet, 1936

As You Like It, 1936

Macbeth, 1948

Hamlet, 1948

Forbidden Planet, 1956

Feature Length Adaptations or Derivatives

The films in this section are based directly or indirectly on plots or characters created by Shakespeare, but are not considered to be strict interpretations of any particular play. The Shakespearean source of each film is indicated.

Hamlet:

To Be or Not To Be

U.S.A. 1942. 99 minutes. Presented by Alexander Korda, released by United Artists. Black and white. 35mm.
Producer and Director: Ernst Lubitsch. **Screenplay:** Edwin Justis Mayer, from an original story by Ernst Lubitsch and Melchior Lengyel. **Photographer:** Rudolph Mate. **Art Director:** Vincent Korda. **Editor:** Dorothy Spencer. **Music:** Werner Heyman.
Cast: Carole Lombard (Maria Tura); Jack Benny (Joseph Tura); Robert Stack (Lieutenant Stanislav Sobinski); Felix Bressart (Greenberg); Lionel Atwill (Rawitch); Stanley Ridges (Professor Siletsky); Sig Rumann (Colonel Ehrhardt); Tom Dugan (Bronski); Charles Halton (Producer Dobosh); George Lynn (Actor-Adjutant); Henry Victor (Captain Schultz); Maude Eburne (Anna); Armand Wright (Makeup Man); Erno Verebes (Stage Manager); Halliwell Hobbes (General Armstrong); Miles Mander (Major Cunningham).
Comment: This now classic film stars Jack Benny as the principal actor in a Polish troupe performing "Hamlet;" there are also some brief renderings from "The Merchant of Venice." Directed by Ernst Lubitsch (who had trained with Max Reinhardt and directed Shakespeare on the stage in Berlin), this anti-Nazi comedy was attacked by critics upon its initial release for being pro-Nazi. Now accepted as a masterpiece of comedy and a prime example of the genius of Lubitsch, the film provided Jack Benny with his best role. Carole Lombard was killed in a plane crash shortly after the film was completed, causing many of her saddened fans to stay away from the picture.

The Rest is Silence

(Der Rest Ist Schweigen)
Germany. 1960. 106 minutes. A Frele Film Production presented by Films Around the World, Inc. Black and white. 35mm.
Producer, Director and Writer: Helmut Kautner.
Cast: Hardy Kruger (John H. Claudius); Peter Van Eyck (Paul Claudius); Ingrid Andree (Fee von Pohl); Adelheid Seeck (Gertrud Claudius); Rudolph Forster (Dr. von Pohl); Boy Gobert (Mike R. Krantz); Rainer Penkert (Major Horace); Heinz Drache (Herbert von Pohl); Charles Regnier (Inspector Fortner); Richard Allan (Stanley Goulden); Robert Meyn (Dr. Voltmann).
Note: English subtitles.

Comment: Another modern day interpretation of the "Hamlet" theme; a young Harvard educated intellectual (Hardy Kruger) feels remorse over the death of his father as well as his family's World War Two industrial profiteering. He is haunted by hallucinatory phone calls from his long dead father, and a passionate love for his mother.

The Bad Sleep Well

Japan. 1963. 135 minutes. Toho. Black and white. 35mm. Tohoscope.
Producers: Tomiyuku Tanaka and Akira Kurosawa. **Director:** Akira Kurosawa. **Screenplay:** Hideo Oguni, Eijiro Hisaita, Ryuzo Kikushima, Shinobu Hashimoto and Kurosawa. **Photographer:** Yuzura Aizawa. **Art Director:** Yoshiro Muraki. **Music:** Masaru Sato.
Cast: Toshiro Mifune (Koichinishi); Tokashi Kato (Ifkaura); Mosayuki Mori (Iwabuchi); Tokashi Shimura (Moriyama); Akira Nishimura (Shirai); Kamatari Fujiwara (Wada); Kyoka Kogawa (Keiko); Tetsuya Miheshi (Tetsue).
Comment: Akira Kurosawa, who had earlier adapted "Macbeth" into *Throne of Blood,* retells the "Hamlet" legend as a tale of corporate immorality and family tragedy. Set in modern-day Japan, this film is a cross between *Executive Suite* and *Scarface.*

Ophelia

France. 1963. 100 minutes. Boreal, released by Trans-Lux Distributing Corp. Black and white. 35mm.
Director and Screenplay: Claude Chabrol. **Literary Collaborator:** Martial Matthieu. **Photographer:** Jean Rabier. **Editor:** Jacques Gaillard. **Music:** Pierre Jansen, conducted by Andre Girard. **Sound:** Jean-Claude Marchetti.
Cast: Alida Valli (Claudia Lesurf); Claude Cerval (Adrien Lesurf); Andre Jocelyn (Yvan Lesurf); Juliette Mayniel (Lucie); Robert Burnier (Andre Lagrange); Jean-Louis Maury (Sparkos); Sacha Briquet (Gravedigger); Liliane David (Ginette); Pierre Vernier (Paul); Serge Bento (Francoise); Roger Carel (Worker); Laszlo Szabo (Foolish Guard); Henri Attal, Dominique Zardi, Jean-Marie Arnoux (Guards).
Note: Location scenes filmed at Villepreux (Yvelines). U.S. release—1964.
Comment: Essentially a film within a film, *Ophelia* tells the tale of a French family, haunted by death, incest, murder and revenge. The film made interesting use of footage from Olivier's *Hamlet,* which had a profound effect on a central character in the story.

Henry VI:

Show of Shows

U.S.A. 1929. 128 minutes. Warner Brothers. Black and white with Technicolor sequences. 35mm.
Director: John Adolfi. **Editor:** Bernard McGill.
Cast ("Henry VI" sequence): John Barrymore (Duke of Gloucester).
Comment: Less than two years after Al Jolson had stunned movie audiences from coast to coast with his *"you ain't heard nothin' yet"* in Warner Brothers' first talkie *The Jazz Singer,* Warners' put its Vitaphone process to a true test with an all-star extravaganza. *Show of Shows* featured everyone Warners' had under contract who could sing, dance, walk, talk, or bark. (Rin-Tin-Tin had part of the action.) Sandwiched into all this, curiously enough, was a stunning performance by John Barrymore as The Duke of Gloucester in his long soliloquy from "Henry

VI." The Barrymore sequences were also shot in an early Technicolor process, but it is not known if those original color separations still exist.

Julius Caesar:

An Honourable Murder

Great Britain. 1960. Running time unknown. Black and white. 35mm.
Producers: Edward J. and Harry Lee Danziger. **Director:** Godfrey Grayson. **Screenplay:** Brian Clemens and Eldon Howard.
Cast: Norman Wooland (Brutus Smith); Margaretta Scott (Claudia Caesar); Lisa Daniely (Paula); Douglas Wilmer (R. Cassius); Philip Saville (Mark Anthony); John Longden (Julian Caesar); Marion Mathie (Portia Smith); Colin Tapley (Casca); Kenneth Edwards (Trebon); Arnold Bell (Ligar).
Comment: Brian Clemens, writer for so many of those witty *The Avengers* shows of the past, co-authored the screenplay of this "Julius Caesar" take-off. As compared to Kurosawa's *The Bad Sleep Well*, *An Honourable Murder* is pure parody, with the chairman of the board of a large corporation losing both the key to the executive washroom and his life in a tale of the corporate purge.

Julius Caesar, Antony and Cleopatra:

Carry on Cleo

Great Britain. 1964. 92 minutes. Anglo Amalgamated Productions, released by Governor Films. Eastman Color. 35mm.
Producer: Peter Rogers. **Director:** Gerald Thomas. **Screenplay:** Talbot Rothwell. **Photographer:** Alan Hume. **Art Director:** Bert Davey. **Editor:** Archie Ludski. **Music:** Eric Rogers. **Sound:** Bill Daniels.
Cast: Sidney James (Mark Antony); Kenneth Williams (Julius Caesar); Kenneth Connor (Hengist Pod); Charles Hawtrey (Seneca); Joan Sims (Calpurnia); Jim Dale (Horsa); Amanda Barrie (Cleopatra); Victor Maddern (Sergeant Major); Julie Stevens (Gloria); Sheila Hancock (Senna Pod); Jon Pertwee (Soothsayer); Francis De Wolff (Agrippa); Michael Ward (Archimedes); Brian Oulton (Brutus); Warren Mitchell (Spencius); David Davenport (Bilius); Tanya Binning (Virginia); Tom Clegg (Sosages); Peter Gilmore (Galley Master); Gertan Klauber (Marcus); Ian Wilson (Messenger); Brian Rawlinson (Hessian Driver); E.V.H. Emmett (Narrator).
Note: U.S. release—1965.
Comment: The producers of *Carry On Cleo* have done for "Julius Caesar" and "Antony and Cleopatra" what they did before to "Romeo and Juliet" (see page 33).   This time, however, history and Shakespeare are both turned around in a bit of black comedy, and Mark Antony plots to assassinate Julius Caesar!

King Lear:

Comment: Shakespearean scholars have frequently listed *Broken Lance* as a Western adaptation of "King Lear." With Spencer Tracy as the grizzly father of feuding children and the husband of an Indian wife, one can make the distinction between *Lear* and *Lance*.

Curiously enough, however, *Broken Lance* is a remake of a 1949 picture, *House of Strangers*, based on a novel by Jerome Weidman. *House of Strangers* featured Edward G. Robinson as the mercurial father/head of an Italian family, which had gone from poverty to wealth in a generation, and had lost much of its integrity in the process.

To add to this puzzle, in 1961, Twentieth Century-Fox, which had produced the earlier two features, released *The Big Show,* a melodrama in the same mold as the other two films. This time, using a circus background, the story concerns a circus owner who pushes his four sons beyond their limits. As is the case with *Broken Lance* and *House of Strangers, The Big Show* is told in flashbacks. Whether all or any of these films are taken from "King Lear" can probably be argued successfully from either position. Only a viewing of the three features by those curious enough to investigate the trio will provide any answer.

Broken Lance

U.S.A. 1954. 96 minutes. Twentieth Century-Fox Film Corporation. Color by DeLuxe. 35 mm. Cinemascope.
Producer: Sol C. Siegel. **Director:** Edward Dmytryk. **Screenplay:** Richard Murphy. **Photographer:** Joe McDonald. **Art Directors:** Lyle Wheeler and Maurice Ransford. **Music:** Leigh Harline.
Cast: Spencer Tracy (Matt Devereaux); Robert Wagner (Joe Devereaux); Richard Widmark (Ben Devereaux); Katy Jurado (Senora Devereaux); Jean Peters (Barbara); Hugh O'Brien (Mike Devereaux); Earl Holliman (Denny Devereaux); Edward Franz (Two Moons); E.G. Marshall (The Governor); Carl Benton Reid (Clem Lawton); Robert Burton (MacAndrews); Philip Ober (Van Cleve); Russell Simpson (Judge); Robert Adler (O'Reilly).

House of Strangers

U.S.A. 1949. 101 minutes. Twentieth Century-Fox Film Corporation. Black and white. 35mm.
Producer: Sol C. Siegel. **Director:** Joseph L. Mankiewicz. **Screenplay:** Philip Yordan, based on a novel by Jerome Weidman. **Photographer:** Milton Krasner. **Art Directors:** Lyle Wheeler and George W. Davis. **Music:** Daniele Amfitheatrof. **Sound:** W.D. Rick and Roger Homan.
Cast: Edward G. Robinson (Gino Monetti); Susan Hayward (Irene Benett); Richard Conte (Max Monetti); Luther Adler (Joe Monetti); Paul Valentine (Pietro Monetti); Efrem Zimbalist, Jr. (Tony); Debra Paget (Maria Domenico); Hope Emerson (Helena Domenico); Esther Miniciotti (Theresa); Diane Douglas (Elaine Monetti); Tito Vuolo (Lucca); Albert Morin (Victorio); Sid Tomack (Walter); Thomas Brown Henry (Judge); David Wolfe (Prosecutor); John Kellogg (Danny); Anne Morrison (Woman Juror).

The Big Show

U.S.A. 1961. 113 minutes. Twentieth Century-Fox Film Corporation. Color by DeLuxe. 35 mm. CinemaScope.
Producers: Ted Sherdeman and James B. Clark. **Director:** James B. Clark. **Screenwriter:** Ted Sherdeman. **Photographer:** Otto Heller. **Music:** Paul Sawtell and Bert Shefter.
Cast: Esther Williams (Hillary); Cliff Robertson (Josef); Nehemiah Persoff (Bruno); Robert Vaughn (Kraus); Carol Christensen (Garda); Margia Dean (Cariotta); Renata Mannhardt (Teresa); David Nelson (Eric); Kurt Fecher (Hans); Franco Andrei (Fredrik); Peter Capell (Vizzini).

Macbeth:

Joe Macbeth
Great Britain. 1955. 90 minutes. Columbia Pictures. Black and white. 35mm.
Producer: M.J. Frankovich. **Director:** Ken Hughes. **Screenplay:** Phillip Yordan.
Cast: Paul Douglas (Joe Macbeth); Ruth Roman (Lily Macbeth); Gregoire Aslan (Duncan—"The Duke"); Sidney James (Banky); Bonar Colleano (Lennie); Minerva Pious (Rosie, the Fortune Teller); Harry Green (Dutch); Teresa Thorne (Ruth).
Comment: This British production was an attempt to adapt "Macbeth" to the gangster genre of the 1930's. Hampered by a low budget, the film is often bleak and tedious. It can be viewed as a curiosity item all right, but Paul Douglas was better off managing the Pittsburgh Pirates in *Angels In The Outfield* than all these New York hoodlums.

Throne of Blood
Japan. 1957. 105 minutes. Brandon Films, Inc. Black and white. 35mm.
Producer and Director: Akira Kurosawa. **Screenplay:** Akira Kurosawa, Shinobu Hashimoto, Ryuzo Kikushima and Hideo Oguni.
Cast: Toshiro Mifune (Taketoki); Isuzu Yamada (Asaji); Takashi Shimura (Noriyasu Odagura); Minoru Chiaki (Yoshiaki); Akira Kubo (Yoshiteru); Takamaru Sasaki (Kuniharu); Yoichi Tachikawa (Kunimaru); Chieko Naniwa (The Weird Woman).
Comment: *Throne of Blood,* an adaptation of "Macbeth," depicts the story of a proud Japanese warrior who is destroyed by ambition, guilt, and that ever-present shadow of the lady of death. The brilliant Toshiro Mifune stars as another man who would be king and director Akira Kurosawa adds his special magic touch to make this film a masterpiece.

Othello:

Men Are Not Gods
Great Britain. 1937. 82 minutes. An Alexander Korda production, released by United Artists. Black and white. 35mm.
Producer: Alexander Korda. **Director:** Walter Reisch. **Scenario:** C.B. Stern, based on a story by Walter Reisch. **Photographer:** Charles Rosher. **Editor:** Henry Cornelius.
Cast: Miriam Hopkins (Ann Williams); Gertrude Lawrence (Barbara); Sebastian Shaw (Edmund Davey); Rex Harrison (Tommy); A.E. Matthews (Skeates); Val Gielgud (The Producer); Laura Smithson (Katherine); Laurence Grossmith (Stanley); Sybil Grove (Painter); Winifred Willard (Mrs. Williams); Wally Patch (Gallery Attendant); James Harcourt (Porter); Rosamund Greenwood (Piano Player); Noel Howlett (Cashier); Paddy Morgan (Kitty); Nicholas Nadegin (Iago); Michael Hogarth (Cassio).
Comment: England's answer to David O. Selznick, Alexander Korda, tried to produce legitimate Shakespearean drama on the screen on a number of occasions and failed. With *Men Are Not Gods,* however, he probably came closest. A high-mannered farce, the film tells the story of a husband-wife acting team (Harrison-Lawrence) who fall into the clutches of a pompous drama critic and a star-struck young woman. Harrison's Othello can be compared, in good fun, to Jack Benny's Hamlet in *To Be Or Not To Be.*

A Double Life

U.S.A. 1947. 104 minutes. A Kanin Production, released by Universal-International. Black and white. 35mm.
Producer: Michael Kanin. **Director:** George Cukor. **Screenwriters:** Ruth Gordon and Garson Kanin. **Photographer:** Milton Krasner. **Art Directors:** Bernard Herzbrun and Harvey Gillett. **Editor:** Robert Parrish. **Music:** Miklos Rozsa. **Sound:** John Austin. **Advisor, "Othello" Sequence:** Walter Hampden.
Cast: Ronald Coleman (Anthony John); Signe Hasso (Brita); Edmond O'Brien (Bill Friend); Shelley Winters (Pat Kroll); Ray Collins (Victor Donian); Phillip Loeb (Max Lasker); Millard Mitchell (Al Cooley); Joe Sawyer (Ray Bonner); Charles LaTorre (Stellini); Whit Bissell (Dr. Stauffer); John Drew Colt (Stage Manager); Peter Thompson (Assistant Stage Manager); Elizabeth Dunne (Gladys); Alan Edmiston (Rex); Art Smith, Sid Tomack (Wigmakers); Wilton Graff (Dr. Mervin); Harlan Briggs (Oscar Bernard); Claire Carleton (Waitress); Betsy Blair, Janet Warren, Marjory Woodworth (Girls in Wig Shop).
Comment: Both a mystery and a melodrama, *A Double Life* features Ronald Coleman as an emotionally disturbed actor who can no longer distinguish between his stage role as Othello and his own self. Coleman received the Academy Award for Best Actor of 1947.

Anna's Sin

(Il Peccato di Anna)
Italy. 1953. 86 minutes. Giaguaro Film, released in U.S. by Atlantis Films. Black and white. 35mm.
Director: Camillo Mastrocinque. **Screenplay:** Edoardo Anton and Camillo Mastrocinque, from a story by Anna Vita. **Photographer:** Alvaro Mancoti. **Editor:** Pier Piccinato and Mario Bonotti (sources conflict in credit). **Music:** Alessandro Cicognini.
Cast: Anna Vita (Anna Curti); Ben E. Johnson (John Ruthford); Paul Muller (Alberto); William Demby (Sam); Pamela Winter (Alley); Giovanna Mazzotti (Laura); Rosario Borelli (Impresario); Oscar Adriani (Michael); Giacomo Rondinella (Singer); Sergio Raimondi; Nino Capozzi; Anna Davila; Marisa Benedetti.
Note: U.S. release of this film—1961.
Comment: Seemingly released in the U.S. as an exploitation potboiler, *Anna's Sin* tells the story of a black American actor (Johnson) who falls in love with a white woman playing Desdemona to his Othello on the Italian stage. As the story progresses, the actor must clear himself of false accusations of rape and murder brought on by an unscrupulous business associate.

Jubal

U.S.A. 1956. 101 minutes. Columbia Pictures. Technicolor. 35mm. CinemaScope.
Producer: William Fadiman. **Director:** Delmar Daves. **Screenplay:** Russell S. Hughes and Delmer Daves, based on a novel by Paul I. Wellman. **Photographer:** Charles Lawton. **Art Director:** Carl Anderson. **Editor:** Al Clark. **Music:** David Raksin. **Sound:** Harry Smith.
Cast: Glenn Ford (Jubal Troop); Ernest Borgnine (Shep Morgan); Rod Steiger (Pinky); Valerie French (Mae Morgan); Felicia Farr (Naomi Hoktor); Basil Ruysdael (Shem Hoktor); Noah Beery, Jr. (Sam); Charles Bronson (Reb Haislipp); John Dierkes (Carson); Jack Elam (McCoy); Robert Burton (Dr. Grant); Robert Knapp (Jake Slavin); Juney Ellis (Charity Hoktor).
Comment: Using "Othello" as its broad story line, *Jubal* tells the story of a tough ranch hand

(Ford) who resists the advances of a married woman (French) whose piano-playing husband (Borgnine) trusts them both. The situation changes for the worse when a rejected suitor (Steiger) takes matters into his hands.

All Night Long

Great Britain. 1962. 91 minutes. Bob Roberts Productions for Rank Organisation; released by Colorama Features. Black and white. 35mm.
Producer: Michael Relph. **Executive Producer:** Bob Roberts. **Director:** Basil Dearden.
Screenplay: Nel King and Peter Achilles. **Photographer:** Ted Scaife. **Art Director:** Ray Simm.
Editor: John D. Guthridge. **Music:** Philip Green. **Sound:** Christopher Lancaster.
Cast: Patrick McGoohan (Johnny Cousin); Marti Stevens (Delia Lane); Betsy Blair (Emily, Johnny's wife); Keith Mitchell (Cass Michaels); Richard Attenborough (Rod Hamilton); Paul Harris (Aurelius Rex); Bernard Braden (Berger); Maria Velasco (Benny); Harry Towb (Phales); Dave Brubeck, John Dankworth, Charles Mingus, Tubby Hayes, Keith Christie, Ray Dempsey, Allan Ganley, Ben Courtley, Barry Morgan, Kenny Napper, Colin Purbrook, Johnny Scott, Geoffrey Holder (Themselves).
Note: U.S. release of this film—1963.
Comment: *All Night Long* takes the Othello theme to a London East End jazz club, where an evil-minded musician (McGoohan) seeks to ruin the interracial marriage of his bandleader (Harris) by spreading vicious rumors about the bandleader's wife (Stevens).

Merry Wives of Windsor, Henry the Fourth, Henry the Fifth:

Falstaff

(Chimes at Midnight)
(Campanadas e Medianoche)
Spain/Switzerland. 1966. 119 minutes. International Films Espagnola Alpine Productions, released in U.S. by Peppercorn-Wormser, Inc., U-M Film Distributors. Black and white. 35mm.
Producers: Emiliano Piedra and Angel Escoloano. **Executive Producer:** Alessandro Tasca.
Director and Screenwriter: Orson Welles. **Photographer:** Edmond Richard. **Art Directors:** Jose Antonio de la Guerra and Mariano Erdorza. **Editor:** Fritz Muller. **Music:** Angelo Francesco Lavagnino, conducted by Pierluigi Urbini.
Cast: Orson Welles (Sir John (Jack) Falstaff); Jeanne Moreau (Doll Tearsheet); Margaret Rutherford (Hostess Quickly); John Gielgud (King Henry IV); Keith Baxter (Prince Hal, later King Henry V); Marina Vlady (Kate Percy); Norman Rodway (Henry Percy, called Hotspur); Alan Webb (Justice Shallow); Walter Chiari (Mr. Silence); Michael Aldridge (Pistol); Tony Beckley (Poins); Fernando Rey (Worcester); Beatrice Welles (Falstaff's page); Andrew Faulds (Westmoreland); Jose Nieto (Northumberland); Jeremy Rowe (Prince John); Paddy Bedford (Bardolph); Ralph Richardson (Narrator).
Note: U.S. release of this film—1967; running time—115 minutes.
Comment: Welles has combined parts of "Henry the Fourth," "Henry the Fifth," and "The Merry Wives of Windsor" to produce this beautiful atmospheric film dealing with the adventures of Sir John Falstaff. Looking somewhat like Monty Woolley in *The Man Who Came to Dinner,* Welles and his supporting cast offer brilliant performances in what is easily Welles' best film of the 1960's.

Richard III:

Tower of London
U.S.A. 1939. 92 minutes. Universal. Black and white. 35mm.
Producer and Director: Rowland V. Lee. **Screenplay:** Robert N. Lee. **Photographer:** George Robinson. **Art Director:** Jack Otterson. **Editor:** Ed Curtiss. **Music:** Charles Previn.
Cast: Basil Rathbone (Richard III); Boris Karloff (Mord); Barbara O'Neil (Elizabeth); Ian Hunter (Edward IV); Vincent Price (Clarence); Nan Grey (Lady Alice Barton); John Sutton (John Wyatt); Leo G. Carroll (Hastings); Miles Mander (Henry VI); Lionel Barrymore (Beacon); Rose Hobart (Anne Neville); Ralph Forbes (Henry Tudor); Frances Robinson (Isobel); Ernest Cossart (Tom Clink); G.P. Huntley (Prince of Wales); John Ridion (DeVere); Ronald Sinclair (Prince Edward); John Herbert-Bond, Donnie Dunagan (Prince Richard).
Comment: Universal and director Rowland V. Lee, fresh from the success of Karloff and Rathbone in *The Son of Frankenstein,* quickly cast the two actors in this historical costume drama in an attempt to cash in on the popularity of their horror series. Audiences, some expecting to see horror, some expecting to see history, got a little of both, with Karloff as a sadistic executioner and Rathbone as a despotic Richard III. Luckily for all of us, Rathbone quickly dropped the cloak of Richard and picked up the one of Sherlock Holmes, protecting us all for a generation to come.

Tower of London
U.S.A. 1962. 79 minutes. Admiral Pictures, released by United Artists. Black and white. 35mm.
Producer: Gene Corman. **Director:** Roger Corman. **Screenplay:** Leo V. Gordon, Amos Powell, James B. Gordon, from a story by Leo V. Gordon and Amos Powell. **Photographer:** Arch R. Daizell. **Art Director:** Daniel Haller. **Editor:** Ronald Sinclair. **Music:** Michael Andersen. **Sound:** Phil Mitchell. **Dialogue Director:** Francis Coppola.
Cast: Vincent Price (Richard of Gloucester); Michael Pate (Sir Ratcliffe); Joan Freeman (Lady Margaret); Robert Brown (Sir Justin); Justice Watson (Edward IV); Sarah Selby (Queen); Richard McCauly (Clarence); Eugene Martin (Edward V); Sandra Knight (Mistress Shore); Richard Hale (Tyrus); Donald Losby (Prince Richard); Bruce Gordon (Earl of Buckingham); Joan Camden (Anne); Sara Taft (Richard of Gloucester's mother).
Comment: Not up to the standard of the 1939 original, this Roger Corman film starred Vincent Price (as Richard) who had become the featured player in most of Corman's drive-in quickies. If for anything, this film should be remembered for Francis Coppola's work as dialogue director, who perhaps thought enough of the sinister goings-on in the script to transfer them four centuries later to *Godfather 1* and *2*.

The Hollywood Revue
U.S.A. 1929. 113 minutes. Metro-Goldwyn-Mayer. Black and white with color sequences. 35mm.
Director: Charles Reisner. **Director—"Romeo and Juliet" Sequence:** Lionel Barrymore. **Dialogue:** Al Boasberg and Robert Hopkins. **Photographers:** John Arnold, I.G. Ries, Maxmillian Fabian. **Editor:** William Gray. **Music:** Arthur Lange. **Dances:** Sammy Lee.
Cast: ("Romeo and Juliet" sequence) John Gilbert (Romeo); Norma Shearer (Juliet).
Comment: M-G-M's answer to Warner Brothers' *Show of Shows*, (see page 26) *Hollywood Revue of 1929* brought out everyone on the Metro lot who had contract obligations. Why

Shakespeare was continually included in these extravaganzas is anyone's guess, but the balcony scene from "Romeo and Juliet" made it into this one. Directed by Lionel Barrymore (John's brother) the scene featured Norma Shearer as Juliet, who would later have the same role in the M-G-M 1936 feature film. The ill-fated John Gilbert, whose career was shattered after sound film made his former female fans laugh at his voice on the screen, played Romeo. Sadder still, Gilbert would die at age 39 of a heart attack, the same year Metro released the full length *Romeo and Juliet* with Leslie Howard cast as Romeo.

Romeo and Juliet:

Romeo and Juliet
Mexico. 1944. Running time unknown. Posa Films, S.A., released by Azteca Films. Black and white. 35mm.
Director: Miguel Delgado. **Screenplay:** Jaime Salvador.
Cast: Cantinflas (Romeo); Elena Marques (Juliet); Jose Baviera (Paris); Andres Soler (Capulet); Emma Roldan (Mme. Capulet); Angel Garasa (Brother Lorenzo); Tito Juneo (Theobold); Ortiz de Zarate (Duke of Verona).
Note: Mexican dialogue, English subtitles.
Comment: Press material suggests this film is a bizarre comedy version of the classic tale. Although undoubtedly in the hands of private collectors, this film is seemingly unavailable for rental.

Carry on Teacher
Great Britain. 1959. 86 minutes. Beaconsfield Films-Anglo Amalgamated Productions, released by Governor Films. Black and white. 35mm.
Producer: Peter Rogers. **Executive Producers:** Nat Cohen and Stuart Levy. **Director:** Gerald Thomas. **Screenplay:** Norman Hudis. **Photographer:** Reginald Wyer. **Art Director:** Alex Vetchinsky, Lionel Couch (sources conflict). **Editor:** John Shirley. **Music:** Bruce Montgomery. **Sound:** Cyril Crowhurst.
Cast: Ted Ray (William Wakefield); Kenneth Connor (Gregory Adams); Leslie Phillips (Alistair Grigg); Charles Hawtrey (Michael Bean); Joan Sims (Sarah Allcock); Kenneth Williams (Edwin Milton); Hattie Jacques (Grace Short); Rosalind Knight (Felicity Wheeler); Cyril Chamberlain (Alf); Richard O'Sullivan (Robin Stevens); Carol White (Sheila Dale); Paul Cole (Atkins); Jane White (Irene); Larry Dann (Boy); Diana Beevers (Penny Lee); George Howell (Billy Haig); Jacqueline Lewis (Pat Gordon); Roy Hines (Harry Bird).
Note: U.S. release of this film—1962.
Comment: A popular school headmaster requests a transfer to a new school. His students, fearing to lose him, arrange for a series of practical jokes which will prevent his transfer. Among other things, a student performance of "Romeo and Juliet" turns into a burlesque show.

Sweet Light in a Dark Room
(Romeo, Juliet and Darkness)
(Romeo, Julie e tma)
Czechoslovakia. 1960. 96 minutes. Barrandor Film Studio for Ceskoslovensky Film, released by Promenade Films. Black and white. 35mm.
Presented by: Moris Ergas, Vlado Hreljanovic, CBK Film Enterprises. **Director:** Jiri Weiss.

Screenplay: Jan Otcenasck and Jiri Weiss. **Photographer:** Vaclav Hanus. **Art Director:** Karel Skvor. **Editor:** Miroslav Hajek. **Music:** Jiri Srnka. **Sound:** Emil Polednik.
Cast: Ivan Mistrik (Pavel); Dana Smutna (Hanka); Jirina Sejbalova (Pavel's mother); Blanka Bohdanova (Kubiasova); Eva Mrazova (Alena); Karla Chadimova (Josefka); Miroslav Svoboda (Wurm); Karlicka Svobodova (Martica Wurmov); Vladimir Raz (Class Master); Milos Nedbal (Headmaster); Anna Meliskova (Kubrychtova); Vaclav Lohnisky (Railwayman); Josef Kozal (Janitor); Ladislav Kazda (Melichar); Jiri Kodet (Vojta); Jindrich Narenta (Bubi) Josef Vorel, Ivo Gubel, Pavel Bartl (Gestapo Agents); Vera Tichankova (Farmer's Wife); Alexandra Myskova (Wurmova).
Note: U.S. release—1966; running time—93 minutes.
Comment: This Czechoslovakian film adapts the Romeo and Juliet characters to the Nazi-occupied Prague of 1942. A Czech student tries to hide a Jewish show girl from the Nazis. Gradually, they fall in love, putting both of their lives in danger.

Romanoff and Juliet
(Dig That Juliet)

U.S.A. 1961. 103 minutes. Pavor, S.A., released by Universal-International. Technicolor. 35mm.
Producer, Director, and Writer: Peter Ustinov. **Photographer:** Robert Krasker. **Art Director:** Alexander Trauner. **Editor:** Renzo Lucidi. **Music:** Mario Naicimbene. **Sound:** Sash Fisher.
Cast: Peter Ustinov (The General); Sandra Dee (Juliet Moulsworth); John Gavin (Igor Romanoff); Akim Tamiroff (Vadim Romanoff); Alix Talton (Beulah Moulsworth); Rik von Nutter (Freddie van der Stuyt); John Phillips (Hooper Moulsworth); Peter Jones (Otto); Tamara Shayne (Evdokia Romanoff); Suzanne Cloutier (Marfa Zlotochienko); Edward Atienza (Patriarch); John Alderson (Randle Wix); Thomas Chalmers (Chief Executive); Carl Don (Spy); Tonio Selwart (President at United Nations); Renato Chiantoni (Joseph the Pilot); Booth Colman (Customs Officer); Moura Budberg (Cook); Ginpaolo Maffei; Strelsa Brown.
Note: Location scenes filmed in Italy.
Comment: The multi-talented Ustinov first presented this sophisticated comedy on the New York stage in 1957. He directed the film version four years later. Ustinov has turned "Romeo and Juliet" into a witty look at Cold War politics and the foolishness of nation turned against nation. Although the romance between an American girl and a Russian boy may seem dated in this post-Watergate era, one must remember the political climate in which it was originally produced to appreciate its true value.

Panic Button

U.S.A. 1964. 90 minutes. Yankee Productions, released by Gorton Associates. Black and white. 35mm.
Producer: Ron Gorton. **Director:** George Sherman. **Screenplay:** Hal Biller. **Adaptation:** Mort Friedman, from an original story by Ron Gorton. **Photographer:** Enzo Serafin. **Music:** Georges Garvarentz.
Cast: Maurice Chevalier (Philippe Fontaine); Eleanor Parker (Louise Harris); Jayne Mansfield (Angela); Michael Connors (Frank Pagano); Akim Tamiroff (Pandowski); Carlo Croccolo (Guido); Vincent Barbi (Mario).
Note: Filmed in Rome and Venice.
Comment: Perhaps a forerunner to Mel Brooks' *The Producers*, *Panic Button* presents the odd tale of a producer (Connors) who tries to produce a preposterous "Romeo and Juliet" in

order to lose money for income tax purposes. With Maurice Chevalier as a has-been actor playing Romeo, and Jayne Mansfield as a talentless Juliet ... oh, well.

The Secret Sex Lives of Romeo and Juliet
(The Secret Love Lives of Romeo and Juliet)
(The Sex Life of Romeo and Juliet)

U.S.A. 1969. 96 minutes. Global Pictures, released by Boxoffice International Film Distributors. Eastman Color. 35mm.
Producer and Director: A.P. Stootsberry. **Screenplay:** Jim Schumacher. **Photographer:** Duane Rayven. **Art Director:** Earl Marshall. **Editor:** Mark Petti.
Cast: Forman Shane (Romeo); Dicora Carse (Juliet); Mickey Jines (Lady Capulet); Stuart Lancaster (Capulet); Adam Lawrence (Montague); Jay Edwards (Balthasar); Wendel Swink (Friar); Vineene Wallace (Nurse); Shannon Carse (The Prince); Don Jones (Gregory); Marvin Sweetbody (Paris); Sydney Carlysle (Derek); Karen Thomas (Maid #1); Pat Davis (Maid #2); Tiffany Lane (Maid #3); Eleanor Rigby (Maid #4); Antoninette Maynard (Maid #5); Dorthea Cristie (Maid #6); Kelly (Stage Hand); James Brand (Narrator).
Comment: An examination of press material for this film indicates the producer may have stayed closer to Shakespeare's story line than other, more literal film versions of the play. Unlike the story as we know it, however, this film has a happy ending!

The Tempest:

Forbidden Planet
U.S.A. 1956. 98 minutes. Metro-Goldwyn-Mayer. Eastman Color. 35mm. CinemaScope.
Producer: Nicholas Nayfack. **Director:** Fred M. Wilcox. **Screenplay:** Cyril Hume, based on a story by Irving Block and Allen Adler. **Photographer:** George J. Folsey. **Art Directors:** Cedric Gibbons and Arthur Lonergan. **Special Effects:** A. Arnold Gillespie, Warren Newcombe, Irving G. Ries, Joshua Meador. **Editor:** Ferris Webster. **Electronic Tonalities:** Louis and Bebe Barron.
Cast: Walter Pidgeon (Dr. Morbius); Anne Francis (Altaira Morbius); Leslie Nielsen (Commander Adams); Warren Stevens (Lieutenant "Doc" Ostrow); Jack Kelly (Lieutenant Farman); Richard Anderson (Chief Quinn); Earl Holliman (Cook); George Wallace (Bosun); Bob Dix (Grey); Jimmy Thompson (Youngerford); James Drury (Strong); Harry Harvey Jr. (Randall); Roger McGee (Lindstrom); Peter Miller (Moran); Morgan Jones (Nichols); Richard Grant (Silvers).
Comment: This surprisingly good science fiction film offers fine performances by everyone and superior special effects from the Walt Disney Studios. The plot surrounds the events on a mysterious planet inhabited only by an aging scientist (Pidgeon) and his daughter (Francis). The arrival of handsome Americans in a space ship creates dissent for the tranquil pair, and a series of horrible murders follow.

Prince of Players
USA. 1955. 102 minutes. Twentieth Century-Fox Film Corp. Color by DeLuxe. 35mm. CinemaScope.
Producer and Director: Philip Dunne. **Screenplay:** Moss Hart, based on the book by Eleanor Ruggles. **Photographer:** Charles G. Clarke. **Art Director:** Lyle Wheeler and Mark-Lee Kirk.

Editor: Dorothy Spencer. **Music:** Bernard Herrmann. **Sound:** Alfred Bruzlin and Harry M. Leonard.
Cast: Richard Burton (Edwin Booth); Maggie McNamara (Mary Devlin); John Derek (John Wilkes Booth); Raymond Massey (Junius Brutus Booth); Charles Bickford (Dave Prescott); Elizabeth Sellers (Asia); Eva LeGallienne (The Queen); Christopher Cook (Edwin Booth—age 10); Dayton Lummis (English Doctor); Ian Keith (King in "Hamlet"); Paul Stader (Laertes); Louis Alexander (John Booth—age 12); William Walker (Old Ben); Jack Raine (Theatre Manager).
Comment: This film is a dramatic interpretation of Eleanor Ruggles' biography of Edwin Booth, who was considered America's greatest Shakespearean actor. Throughout the film, as Booth's life is re-created, a number of passages of different works of Shakespeare are presented in a "play within a play" format. These include Richard Burton (as Booth) in parts of "Richard III," "Hamlet," and "Romeo and Juliet;" also, Raymond Massey (as Booth's father, Junius Brutus Booth) in scenes from "King Lear" and "Twelfth Night."

To Be Or Not To Be, 1942

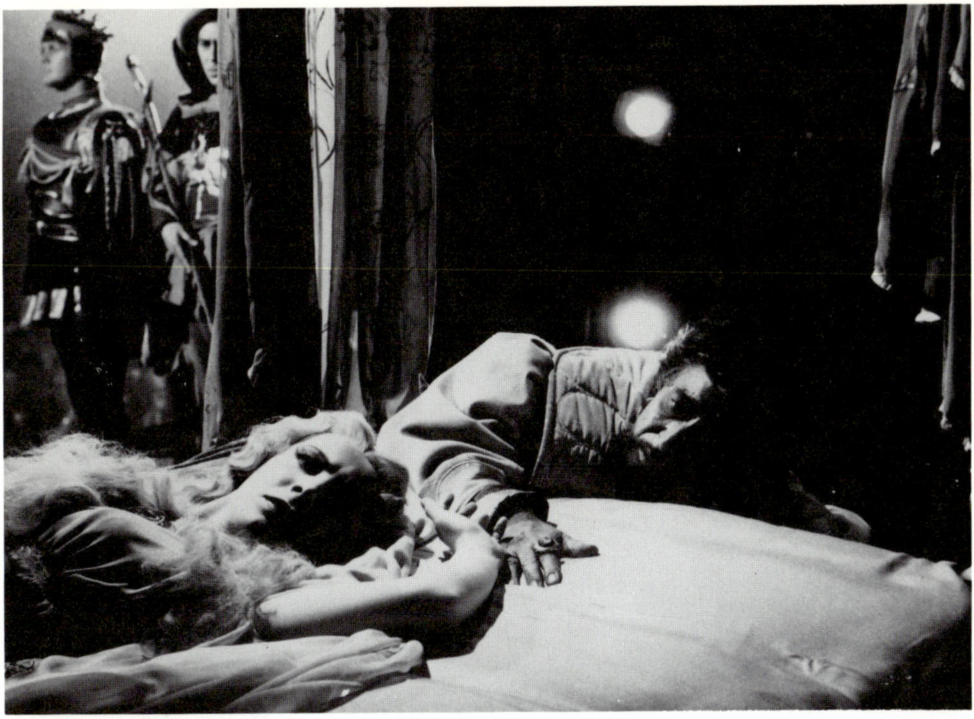

A Double Life, 1947

Tower of London, 1939

37

Othello, 1952

Forbidden Planet, 1956

Broken Lance, 1954

39

Kiss Me Kate, 1953

Dance, Musical, or Operatic Versions:

Each film in this section is based either directly or abstractly on a particular work by Shakespeare. In many cases the story line is intact, but music or dance has been added (e.g. *Ballet of Romeo and Juliet* or the German opera, *The Merry Wives of Windsor.*) In other cases, a plot line has been borrowed and changed substantially (e.g. "The Taming of the Shrew"/*Kiss Me Kate.*) For the most part, the title of the dance, musical or opera film is the same as its play source; where it is not, the Shakespearean source has been indicated.

The Boys from Syracuse
(Musical comedy adaptation of "The Comedy of Errors")
U.S.A. 1940. 73 minutes. Universal Studios. Black and white. 35mm.
Producer: Jules Levey. **Director:** A. Edward Sutherland. **Screenplay:** Leonard Spiegelgass and Charles Grayson; based on the musical comedy by George Abbott, Richard Rodgers and Lorenz Hart. **Photographer:** Joseph Valentine. **Editor:** Milton Carruth. **Music:** Richard Rodgers and Lorenz Hart.
Cast: Allan Jones (Antipholus of Ephesus, Antipholus of Syracuse); Martha Raye (Luce); Joe Penner (Dromio of Ephesus, Dromio of Syracuse); Rosemary Lane (Phyllis); Charles Butterworth (Duke of Ephesus); Irene Hervey (Adriana); Alan Mowbray (Angelo); Eric Blore (Pinch); Samuel S. Hinds (Aegeon).

The Merry Wives of Windsor
(Operatic adaptation of "The Merry Wives of Windsor")
Germany. 1952. Running time unknown. Deutsche Film A.G., released by Central Cinema Corporation. Black and white. 35mm.
Producer: Walter Lehmann. **Director:** Georg Wildhagen. **Screenplay:** Wolff von Gordon and Georg Wildhagen, based on the play by William Shakespeare and the opera by Otto Nicolai. **Music:** Otto Nicolai, played by the Orchestra of the Berlin State Opera.
Cast: Sonja Ziemann (Frau Fluth—Mrs. Ford); Camilla Spira (Frau Reich—Mrs. Page); Paul Esser (Sir John Falstaff); Claus Holm (Herr Fluth—Mr. Ford); Alexander Engel (Herr Reich—Mr. Page); Eckart Dux (Fenton); Ina Halley (Anna Reich—Anne Page); Joachim Teege (Herr Spaerlich—Slender); Gerhard Frickhoffer (Dr. Cajus).
Note: This film is sung in German, with English subtitles.

The Merry Wives of Windsor
(Die lustigen weiber von Windsor)
(Operatic adaptation of "The Merry Wives of Windsor")

Austria. 1965. 97 minutes. Wien Film, released in the U.S. by Sigma III Corp. Technicolor. 35mm.
Producer: Norman Foster. **Director:** George Tressler. **Screenplay and English Adaptation of German Libretto:** Norman Foster, from an opera by Otto Nicolai based on the Shakespeare play. **Photographer:** Hannes Staudinger. **Art Director:** Hugo Halbig. **Editor:** Paula Dvorak. **Music:** Otto Nicolai, performed by the Zagreb Symphony Orchestra, conducted by Milan Horvath. **Choreographer:** Rosella Hightower.
Cast: Norman Foster (Sir John Falstaff); Colette Boky (Frau Fluth—Mistress Ford); Igor Gorin (Herr Fluth—Mr. Ford); Mildred Miler (Frau Reich—Mistress Page); Edmond Hurshell (Herr Reich—Master Page); Lucia Popp (Anna—Mistress Ann); Ernst Shutz (Fenton); John Gittings (Cajus); Marshall Raynor (Sparlich); Rosella Hightower (Ballerina).
Note: U.S. release of this film—1966.

A Midsummer Night's Dream
(Ballet adaptation of "A Midsummer Night's Dream")

U.S.A. 1967. 93 minutes. Oberon Productions, released by Columbia Pictures. Eastman Color by Pathe. 35mm. Panavision.
Producer: Richard Davis. **Director:** Dan Eriksen. **Production Conception:** George Balanchine. **Photographer:** Arthur J. Ornitz. **Art Director:** Albert Brenner. **Editor:** Armond Lebowitz. **Music:** Felix Mendelssohn; played by the Orchestra of the New York City Ballet, conducted by Robert Irving. **Choreographer:** George Balanchine.
Cast: Suzanne Farrell (Titania); Edward Villella (Oberon); Arthur Mitchell (Puck); Mimi Paul (Helena); Nicholas Magallanes (Lysander); Patricia McBride (Hermia); Roland Vazquez (Demetrius); Francisco Moncion (Theseus); Gloria Govrin (Hippolyta); Richard Rapp (Bottom); Jacques D'Amboise (Court Danseur); Allegra Kent (Court Danseuse); The New York City Ballet and the Children of the School of American Ballet.
Note: The opening of the film was a special benefit showing released by Columbia Pictures in association with the City Center of Music and Drama, Inc. Subsequent release was by Showcorporation with the sponsorship of *McCall's Magazine*.

The Moor's Pavane
(Ballet adaptation of "Othello")

1950. 16 minutes. Color. 35mm.
Director: Walter V. Strate. **Music:** Henry Purcell. **Choreographer:** Jose Limon. **Dancers:** Jose Limon; Lucas Hoving; Betty Jones; Ruth Currier; Doris Humphrey.
Note: *The Moor's Pavane* is a ballet film based on "Othello." It features the Jose Limon Dance Troupe performing throughout. The complete film runs 16 minutes; it has not been edited from another feature.

Ballet of Othello
(Ballet adaptation of "Othello")

USSR. 1960. 95 minutes. Gruziya-Film, released in U.S. by Artkino Pictures. Sovcolor. 35mm.
Director: Vakhtang Chabukiani. **Screenplay:** Yuriy Gelovani and Vakhtang Chabukiani. **Photographer:** Feliks Vysotskiy. **Art Director:** Serapion Vatsadze and Solomon Virsaladze.

Music: Aleksey Machavariani. **Sound:** D. Lomidze. **Ballet Master:** Vakhtang Chabukiani.
Cast: Vakhtang Chabukiani (Othello); Vera Tsignadze (Desdemona); Zurab Kikaleyshvili (Iago); Eteri Chabukiani (Bianca); Liana Mitayshvili (Emilia); B. Manavardisashvili (Cassio); R. Tsulukidze (Roderigo); Mikhail Dudko (Brabantio); M. Gelyus (Montano); V. Ivashkin (Duke of Venice); featuring the Paliashvili Opera Theatre and Ballet of Tbilisi.
Note: U.S. release—1964.

Catch My Soul
(Santa Fe Satan)
(Musical adaptation of "Othello")
U.S.A. 1973. 100 minutes. Metromedia Producers Corp. Color. 35mm.
Executive Producer: Charles Fries. **Director:** Patrick McGoohan. **Screenplay:** Jack Good. **Photographer:** Conrad Hall. **Editor:** Richard A. Harris. **Music Producer and Arranger:** Delaney Bramlett. **Background Music Score:** Tony Joe White.
Cast: Richie Havens (Othello); Lance Le Gault (Iago); Season Hubley (Desdemona); Tony Joe White (Cassio); Susan Tyrrell (Emilia).
Note: Patrick McGoohan, who startled American TV audiences with his *Secret Agent* and *The Prisoner* shows of the late 1960's, directed this often confusing rock opera version of "Othello." Set in a desert hippie commune outside Santa Fe, New Mexico, *Catch My Soul* often imitated the then popular *Jesus Christ, Superstar;* however, that touch just doesn't work here. McGoohan was in another "Othello" adaptation, *All Night Long*, in which he played marriage wrecker as well as the drums.

The Ballet of Romeo and Juliet
(Ballet adaptation of "Romeo and Juliet")
USSR. 1954. 96 minutes. A Mosfilm Production, released by Tohan Pictures Company. Magicolor. 35mm.
Producer: Leonid Lavrovsky. **Directors and Screenwriters:** Lev Arnshtam and Leonid Lavrovsky. **Photographers:** Alexander Shelenkov and Chen Yu-Lan. **Art Director:** Alexei Perkhomenko. **Music:** Sergei Prokofiev; played by the Orchestra of the Bolshoi Theatre, conducted by Gennadi Rozhdestvensky. **Choreographer:** Leonid Lavrovsky.
Cast: Galina Ulanov (Juliet); Yuri Zhdanov (Romeo); Alexei Yermolayev (Tybalt); Sergei Koren (Mercutio); Alexander Lapauri (Paris); Alexander Radunsky (Capulet); Yelena Illuschenka (Lady Capulet); Iraida Olenina (Juliet's Nurse); Lev Loschilin (Friar Laurence); Georgi Farmalantz (Clown); and the Dancers and Corps de Ballet of The Bolshoi Theatre.
Note: This film won the Grand Prize at the 1955 Cannes Film Festival.

West Side Story
(Musical adaptation of "Romeo and Juliet")
U.S.A. 1961. 155 minutes. Mirish Pictures-Seven Arts Productions-Beta Productions, released by United Artists. Technicolor. 35mm and 70mm. Westrex Sound. Panavision 70.
Producer: Robert Wise. **Directors:** Robert Wise and Jerome Robbins. **Screenplay:** Ernest Lehmann. **Photographer:** Daniel L. Fapp. **Photographic Effects:** Linwood Dunn, Film Effects of Hollywood. **Production Design:** Boris Leven. **Editor:** Thomas Stanford. **Music:** Leonard Bernstein; Lyrics: Stephen Sondheim; Conducted by Johnny Green. **Sound:** Murray Spievack, Fred Lau, Vinton Vernon. **Sound Editor:** Gilbert D. Marchant. **Choreographer:** Jerome Robbins.

Cast: Natalie Wood (Maria); Richard Beymer (Tony); Russ Tamblyn (Riff); Rita Moreno (Anita); George Chakiris (Bernardo); Simon Oakland (Lieutenant Schrank); Ned Glass (Doc); William Bramley (Officer Krupke); John Astin (Glad Hand, a social worker); Penny Santon (Madam Lucia); Singing voice for Natalia Wood (uncredited) Marnie Nixon; Singing voice for Richard Beymer (uncredited) Jimmy Bryant.
Note: This film is based on the Arthur Laurents-Leonard Bernstein Broadway musical play.

Los Tarantos
(Musical drama adaptation of "Romeo and Juliet")

Spain. 1964. 91 minutes. Tecisa, released in U.S. by Sigma III Corporation. Eastman Color. 35mm.
Producers: Jose G. Maesso and Leonard Gruenberg. **Director:** Rovira-Beleta. **Screenplay:** Rovira-Beleta and Alfredo Manas. **Photographer:** Massimo Dallamano. **Art Director:** Juan Alberto Soler. **Editor:** Emilio Rodriguez Oses. **Music:** Emilio Pujol, Fernando Garcia Morcillo, Andres Batista, Jose Sola.
Cast: Carmen Amaya (Augustias); Sara Lezana (Juana); Daniel Martin (Rafael); Antonio Prieto (Rosendo); Margarita Lozano (Isabel); Jose Manuel Martin (Curro); Antonio Gades (Mojigongo); Antonia Singla (Sole); Aurelio Amapola Garcia (Antonia); Rosario Ortiz (Aurora); Antonio Lavilla (Sancho); Anselmo Batista and Andres Batista (Picaos); Antonio Guisa (Friend of the Picaos); Carmen Amaya Co. (Flamenco Dancers).
Note: Released in the United States three years after *West Side Story* was so successful, this Spanish-made film has attracted a wide following among film cultists. Also a musical-drama, *Los Tarantos* is set in torrid Barcelona, with family pitted against family, except for the timeless star-crossed lovers.

Romeo and Juliet
(Ballet adaptation of "Romeo and Juliet")

Great Britain. 1966. 126 minutes. Poetic Films, released by Embassy Pictures. Eastman color, print by Pathe. 35mm.
Producer and Director: Paul Czinner. **Photographer:** S.D. Onions. **Editor:** Philip Barnickel. **Music:** Sergei Prokofiev, played by Orchestra of the Royal Opera House (Covent Garden), conducted by John Lanchberry. **Choreographer:** Kenneth MacMillan.
Cast: Margot Fonteyn (Juliet); Rudolf Nureyev (Romeo); David Blair (Mercutio); Desmond Doyle (Tybalt); Anthony Dowell (Benvolio); Derek Rencher (Paris); Michael Somes (Lord Capulet); Julia Farron (Lady Capulet); Leslie Edwards (Escalus, Prince of Verona); Georgina Parkinson (Rosaline); Gerd Larsen (Nurse); Ronald Hund (Friar Laurence); Christopher Newton (Lord Montague); Betty Kavanagh (Lady Montague); the Royal Ballet Company.
Note: Prokofiev's ballet, *Romeo and Juliet,* as choreographed by Kenneth MacMillan premiered at the London Royal Opera House on February 9, 1965. The film was made in a studio during a stage performance with the entire stage cast present and used original costumes and settings.

Kiss Me Kate
(Musical comedy adaptation of "The Taming of the Shrew")

U.S.A. 1953. 109 minutes. Metro-Goldwyn-Mayer. Technicolor. 35mm.
Producer: Jack Cummings. **Director:** George Sidney. **Screenplay:** Dorothy Kingsley; from the play by Samuel and Bella Spewack. **Photographer:** Charles Rosher. **Art Directors:** Cedric

Gibbons and Urie McLeary. **Editor:** Ralph E. Winters. **Music and Lyrics:** Cole Porter. **Musical Directors:** Andre Previn and Saul Chapin. **Sound:** Douglas Shearer. **Choreographer:** Hermes Pan.
Cast: Kathryn Grayson (Lilli Vanessi); Howard Keel (Fred Graham); Ann Miller (Lois Lane); Keenan Wynn (Lippy); Bobby Van ("Gremio"); Tommy Rall (Bill Calhoun); James Whitmore (Slug); Kurt Kaszner ("Baptista"); Bob Fosse ("Hortensio"); Ron Randell (Cole Porter); Willard Parker (Tex Callaway); Dave O'Brien (Ralph); Claud Allister (Paul); Ann Codee (Suzanne); Carol Haney, Jeanne Coyne (Specialty Dancers).
Note: This film was released in 3-D format, in addition to the conventional format.

West Side Story, 1961

Hamlet, National Geographic Series

Educational, Instructional, and Abridged Versions

All films listed in this section were developed for instructional purposes, and are not feature length theatrical releases.

In an effort to broaden the listing of films available for classroom use, this section will provide information on a series of short subject films dealing with Shakespeare or abridgements of Shakespeare's works. It is not intended to be a complete or exhaustive listing of all educational films available, nor is it meant to exclude the mention of a particular film or films.

As film and video become more and more a part of educational cirricula, the availability and marketing of short subjects has increased dramatically. Therefore, we encourage those interested in viewing abbreviated versions of Shakespeare's plays, or educational and documentary films dealing with Shakespeare to contact their local public library system, area universities, as well as civic and religious organizations to determine the availability of classroom films. Often, many of these institutions handle these films free of charge or for a minimal fee.

I further suggest you consult the following educational film directories for a more specific listing of other possible titles:

Educational Film Locator, Published by R.R. Bowker Company; 1180 Avenue of the Americas; New York, New York 10036.

Index to 16mm Educational Films, Published by National Information Center for Educational Media, University of Southern California; University Park; Los Angeles, California 90007.

Index to Instructional Media Catalogs, Published by R.R. Bowker Company; 1180 Avenue of the Americas; New York, New York 10036.

The National Geographic Series: "The World of William Shakespeare"

Seven films dealing with the works and life of Shakespeare. "Hamlet," "Macbeth," and "Romeo and Juliet" are presented in abridged 35 minute editions; each is accompanied by a 25 minute film which offers an examination of the play itself and the historical conditions under which Shakespeare wrote it. All films in the series are: directed by Bob Walsh; produced in 1978; 16mm; color.

Additional information may be obtained by writing: The National Geographic Society, Educational Services, Washington, D.C. 20036.

The titles in the series are:

Hamlet
The Time Is Out of Joint
(interpretation of "Hamlet")

Macbeth
Fair Is Foul, and Foul Is Fair
(interpretation of "Macbeth")

Romeo and Juliet
Star Crossed Love
(interpretation of "Romeo and Juliet")
Shakespeare of Stratford and London
A 35 minute film offering insight into Shakespeare's life and times; filmed on location in London.

The International Film Bureau Series: "The Shakespeare Series"

Twelve films that offer scenes or excerpts from a specific work of Shakespeare. All films in the series are: directed by Peter Seabourne; 16mm; color.
For additional information, contact: International Film Bureau, 332 South Michigan Avenue, Chicago, Illinois 60604.
In Canada, contact: Educational Film Distributors, Ltd., 285 Lesmill Road, Don Mills, Ontario M3B 2Vl.

The titles in the series are:
Antony and Cleopatra
11 minutes. Excerpts from Act II, scene ii and Act V, scene ii.
Hamlet
10 minutes. Excerpts from Act I, scene iv and Act V, scene i.
Henry IV (Part 2)
5½ minutes. Excerpts from Act II, scene ii.
Julius Caesar
14 minutes. Excerpts from Act II, scene ii and Act IV, scene iii.
Macbeth
11 minutes. Excerpts from Act I, scene i, Act I, scene iii, Act IV, scene i, and Act II, scene i.
Much Ado About Nothing
11½ minutes. Excerpts from Act II, scene i and Act V, scene ii.
Othello
9½ minutes. Excerpts from Act II, scene i and Act V, scene ii.
Richard II
12 minutes. Excerpts from Act II, scene i and Act V, scene v.
Richard III
11½ minutes. Excerpts from Act I, scene i and Act I, scene ii.
Romeo and Juliet
8 minutes. Excerpts from The Prologue and Act V, scene iii.
The Taming of the Shrew
13 minutes. Excerpts from Act I, scene ii and Act II, scene i.
The Tempest
13½ minutes. Excerpts from Act I, scene ii and Act III, scene i.

The Westinghouse Series: "The Fair Adventure Series"

Seven 28-minute instructional films, which provide insight into Shakespeare's life and times; plus ten abridged versions of Shakespearean plays. All of the films are: produced by the Westinghouse Broadcasting Company; black and white; 16mm.

The seven 28-minute films are introduced and narrated by Dr. Frank Baxter of the University of California. For additional information, contact: Audio Brandon Films/Macmillan Films Inc., 34 MacQuesten Parkway South, Mount Vernon, New York 10550.

Instructional films:

Shakespeare's World and Shakespeare's London
An explanation of Renaissance England and its effect on Shakespeare.

How To Read A Shakespeare Play
An outline of a basic approach to understanding Shakespeare's writing.

Kings and Queens
Information on the historical periods dealt with in Shakespeare's plays.

The Life of William Shakespeare
A biography of Shakespeare.

The Printing of The Plays
A discussion of the way in which Shakespeare's works were printed.

Shakespeare's Stratford
A study of the atmosphere of Stratford-on-Avon, where Shakespeare lived, and its influence on his works.

Shakespeare's Theater
A look into the original staging of Shakespeare's plays and a study of the Globe Theater.

Plays by Shakespeare:

Much Ado About Nothing
84 minutes; 3 part abridged version.

Twelfth Night
84 minutes; 3 part abridged version.

The Tempest
112 minutes; 4 part abridged version.

Henry V
84 minutes; 3 part abridged version.

Richard II
112 minutes; 4 part abridged version.

Richard III
112 minutes; 4 part abridged version.

Romeo and Juliet
140 minutes; 5 part abridged version.

King Lear
140 minutes; 5 part abridged version.

Macbeth
140 minutes; 5 part abridged version.

Othello
140 minutes; 5 part abridged version.

The Encyclopaedia Britannica Series: "The Humanities Series"

Ten films: Four deal with "Hamlet," three with "Macbeth," and three with the writings of Shakespeare versus those of George Bernard Shaw. All films are color; 16mm. For additional information contact: Encyclopaedia Britannica Educational Corporation, 425 North Michigan Avenue, Chicago, Illinois 60611.

"Hamlet"

Hamlet: The Age of Elizabeth
30 minutes. A discussion of the classes and customs of the Elizabethan Age, as well as the theater of that period.

What Happens In Hamlet
30 minutes. An interpretation of Hamlet as a ghost story, a revenge story, and a mystery.

Hamlet: The Poisoned Kingdom
30 minutes. A discussion of Hamlet as the story of a ruined kingdom.

Hamlet: The Readiness Is All
30 minutes. A discussion of Hamlet from the viewpoint of a man coming of age and discovering reality.

"Macbeth"

Macbeth: The Politics of Power
28 minutes. An interpretation of the characters in Macbeth.

Macbeth: The Themes of Macbeth
28 minutes. An examination of the paradoxes of Macbeth.

Macbeth: The Secret'st Man
33 minutes. A discussion of the good and evil that can exist in all people.

"Shakespeare Versus Shaw"

In this three film series, Donald Moffatt portrays George Bernard Shaw.

Shaw vs. Shakespeare: The Character of Caesar
35 minutes. George Bernard Shaw discusses his interpretation of Caesar in "Caesar and Cleopatra" as compared to Shakespeare's Caesar in "Julius Caesar."

Shaw vs. Shakespeare: The Tragedy of Julius Caesar
35 minutes. Shaw discusses the problem of political idealism and its relationship to Caesar's death.

Shaw vs. Shakespeare: Caesar and Cleopatra
33 minutes. Shaw continues his discussion, this time focusing on the progress of the human race.

Romeo and Juliet, National Geographic Series

Macbeth, National Geographic Series

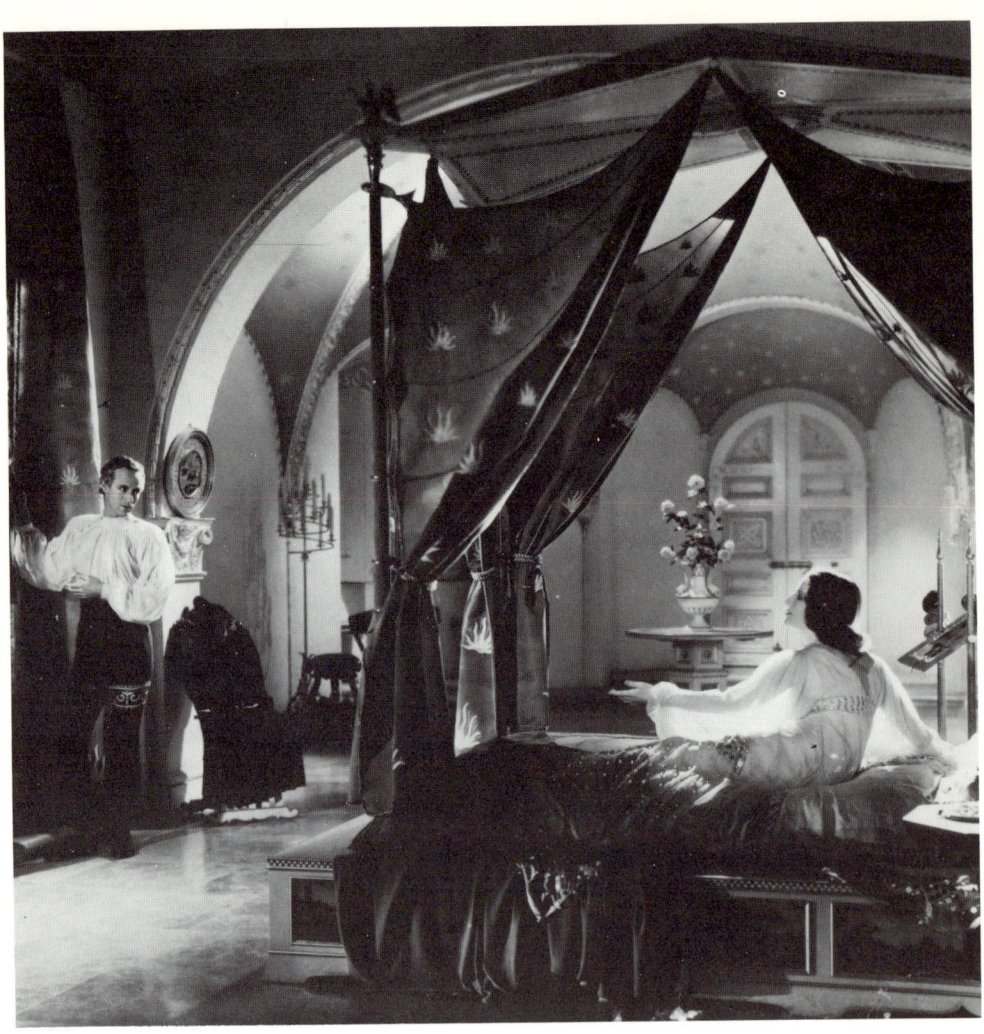
Romeo and Juliet, 1936

Appendix I
Incidentals

Test Shots for Hamlet

John Barrymore, considered by many to be the finest Shakespearean actor since Edwin Booth, was approached in 1933 to do a film version of "Hamlet." Despite the fact that Barrymore had played the part on stage throughout the world, and had already done any number of pictures in Hollywood, the financer for the film demanded a screen test, perhaps due to rumors of Barrymore's unsound health and failing memory. In December, 1933, Barrymore was tested for the screen version of *Hamlet* at R.K.O. Studios in Hollywood. Although his performance was flawless in part of the test, he could not remember his lines in another key scene (Act I, scene v). Worried that the expensive Technicolor production might fail with Barrymore, the producers of the film abandoned the *Hamlet* project. Fortunately, the Test Shost were saved by the principal investor of the film, John Hay Whitney, and restored by The Museum of Modern Art Department of Film.

U.S.A. 10 minutes. Technicolor. 35mm.
Director: Robert Edmond Jones and Margaret Carrington. Produced at R.K.O. (Radio) Studios in December, 1933.
Cast: John Barrymore (Hamlet); Irving Pichel; Reginald Denny; Donald Crisp.

Macbeth

U.S.A. 1951. 78 minutes. Produced by Unusual Films at Bob Jones University, South Carolina. 16mm.
Director: Katherine Stenholm. **Production Supervisor:** Melvin Stratton. **Photographer:** Bob Craig. **Editor:** Ralph Nichols. **Music:** Richard Girvin; played by The Bob Jones University Orchestra.
Note: This version of "Macbeth" was produced at Bob Jones University in Greenville, South Carolina. The university has presented a number of successful stage ventures over the years and in 1950 had an early film production program. Although never shown theatrically, this film has reached a large audience via classroom and university showings over the years.

The Taming of the Shrew, 1929

Appendix II
Additional Listing of Films Representing Shakespeare

In addition to the motion pictures mentioned previously in this filmography, a number of additional features making use of the writings and/or characters created by Shakespeare have been produced over the years. These additional titles were not included beforehand either because they were too cursory in their approach to Shakespeare or too unrelated to any specific (Shakespearean) work for serious scholarly study. However, all these films, as unusual as some of them might be, are but another example of the effect Shakespeare has had on the screen. Shakespearean scholars might well find them entertaining as well as informative.

Morning Glory (R.K.O., 1933) starred a young Katharine Hepburn as an over-ambitious actress seeking to impress a prominent producer. After an evening of too much drinking, she performs the "to be or not to be" soliloquy from "Hamlet." *Morning Glory* was remade in 1958, this time with Susan Strasberg in the title role (R.K.O., 1958). Some similar scenes from "Hamlet" were included.

Thelma Todd, the ravishing blonde who died tragically in 1935, played a Katherina ("Taming of the Shrew") type character in a British comedy entitled *You Made Me Love You* (Majestic Pictures, 1934) which a *New York Times* critic called "too violent for comfort or comedy." The 1930's also produced *The Great Garrick* (Warner Brothers, 1937) in which Brian Ahern played David Garrick, hero of the 18th century theater. Parts of "Hamlet" were included in the film. A couple of comedy ventures, *It's Love I'm After* (Warner Brothers, 1937) and *That's Right, You're Wrong* (R.K.O., 1939), saw the likes of Bette Davis, Leslie Howard, Kay Kyser and Lucille Ball in bits spoofing "Romeo and Juliet." Leslie Howard also quoted from "Richard II" in his role as *The Scarlet Pimpernel* (Korda, 1935).

John Barrymore, whose tragic career was nearing an end by the 1940's (see Appendix I) was hamming it up in two potboilers, *The Great Profile* (Fox, 1940) and *Playmates* (R.K.O., 1941) in which he played a Shakespearean actor caricaturing himself. *Stage Door Canteen* (United Artists 1943) was an all-star show put together for servicemen and featuring Lon McCallister and Katherine Cornell in a bit of "Romeo and Juliet." *Presenting Lilly Mars* (M-G-M, 1943) gave Judy Garland a chance to do a portion of "Macbeth," while *Roseanna McCoy* (R.K.O., 1949) saw the Hatfield and McCoy legend given the "Romeo and Juliet" treatment, with Farley Granger and Joan Evans as the lovers. Another oddity from the 40's is a film called *Strange Illusion* (P.R.C. Pictures, 1945), directed by the gifted Edgar G. Ulmer. *Strange Illusion* is yet another offshoot of "Hamlet," in which the central characters are beset by family troubles.

Two post-war French films, *The Lovers of Verona* (1948) and *The Strange Desire of Monsieur Bard* (1953), dealt with "Romeo and Juliet" and "The Merchant of Venice," respectively. John Barrymore was brought back to life (portrayed by Errol Flynn) as a central character in *Too Much, Too Soon* (Warner Brothers, 1958), the story of the tragic life of

Barrymore's daughter, Diana. Flynn, as Barrymore, recites various passages from Shakespeare from time to time in the film. Producer Irwin Allen, known today for his disaster pictures (*The Towering Inferno*), cranked out a good versus evil epic in 1957 entitled *The Story of Mankind* (Warner Brothers). Besides reuniting The Marx Brothers for the first time in years, the film featured Reginald Gardiner in the role of The Bard himself.

Ralph Richardson and Jason Robards taunted one another with Shakespearean passages in Sidney Lumet's film adaptation of Eugene O'Neill's *Long Day's Journey Into Night* (Embassy, 1962), probably the best film version of any O'Neill play. Jon Voight played a teen-age bully in *Out of It* (United Artists, 1969), which deals with the problems of four Long Island teenagers liberated from high school but confused about their future lives. A part of a performance of "Romeo and Juliet" is featured in the film, and one could suggest that the plot of the film draws some parallels. The remake of *The Charge of the Light Brigade* (United Artists, 1968) had the distinguished British actor, Donald Wolfit, performing "Macbeth" to a less than receptive audience. A 1969 Indian film, *Shakespeare Wallah,* saw a British Shakespearean acting troupe making their way through the back roads of India where they develop motor trouble. Rescued by a handsome Indian, a romance develops between the Indian and the daughter of the head of the troupe. And for those of you who just love a good villain, Vincent Price is as bad as they come in *Theater of Blood* (United Artists, 1973) in which he portrays a psychotic Shakespearean actor murdering his enemies in the fashion described in particular works of the master, something that hopefully won't become a fad.

Hamlet, 1948

King Lear (Korol' Lir), 1970

Suggested Readings

Shakespeare on Silent Film, by Robert Hamilton Ball, 1968, Theater Arts Books, 333 Sixth Avenue, New York, New York 10014.

Shakespeare on Film, by Peter Morris, 1972, Canadian Film Institute, 75 Albert, Suite 1105, Ottawa K1P 5E7 Ontario, Canada.

Shakespeare on Film, by Jack J. Jorgens, 1977, Indiana University Press, Bloomington, Indiana 47401.

Focus on Shakespearean Films, edited by Charles W. Eckert, 1972 (out of print), Film Focus Series, published by Prentice-Hall, Inc., Englewood Cliffs, New Jersey 07632.

Shakespeare and the Film, by Roger Manuell, 1978, A.S. Barnes and Company, Inc., Cranbury, New Jersey 08512.

Shakespeare on Film Newsletter, edited by Bernice W. Kliman and Kenneth S. Rothwell, % The Department of English, University of Vermont, Burlington, Vermont 05405. Published twice a year. Subscriptions: $2 annually.

A Double Life, 1947

Index

All Night Long, 31
An Honorable Murder, 27
Anna's Sin, 30
Antony and Cleopatra (1973), 11
Antony and Cleopatra (International Film Bureau Series), 48
As You Like It, 11

Bad Sleep Well, The, 26
Ballet of Othello, 42
Ballet of Romeo and Juliet, The, 43
Big Show, The, 28
Boys From Syracuse, The, 41
Broken Lance, 28

Carry on Cleo, 27
Carry on Teacher, 33
Catch My Soul, 43

Double Life, A, 30

Fair Is Foul, and Foul Is Fair, 47
Falstaff (Chimes at Midnight), 31
Forbidden Planet, 35

Hamlet (1948), 11
Hamlet (1960), 12
Hamlet (1964—U.S.A.), 12
Hamlet (1964—U.S.S.R.), 12
Hamlet (1970), 13
Hamlet (International Film Bureau Series), 48
Hamlet (National Geographic Series), 47
Hamlet: The Age of Shakespeare, 50
Hamlet: The Poisoned Kingdom, 50
Hamlet: The Readiness Is All, 50
Henry IV, 48
Henry V (1944), 13
Henry V (Fair Adventure Series), 49
Hollywood Revue, The, 32
House of Strangers, 28
How To Read A Shakespeare Play, 49

Joe Macbeth, 29
Jubal, 30
Julius Caesar (1950), 13
Julius Caesar (1953), 14
Julius Caesar (1970), 14

Julius Caesar (International Film Bureau Series), 48

King Lear (1970—Great Britain), 14
King Lear (1970—U.S.S.R.), 15
King Lear (Fair Adventure Series), 49
Kings and Queens, 49
Kiss Me Kate, 44

Life of William Shakespeare, The, 49
Los Tarantos, 44

Macbeth (1946), 15
Macbeth (1948), 15
Macbeth (1951), 53
Macbeth (1960), 16
Macbeth (1971), 16
Macbeth (Fair Adventure Series), 49
Macbeth (International Film Bureau Series), 48
Macbeth (National Geographic Series), 47
Macbeth: The Politics of Power, 50
Macbeth: The Secret'st Man, 50
Macbeth: The Themes of Macbeth, 50
Men Are Not Gods, 29
Merry Wives of Windsor, The (1952), 41
Merry Wives of Windsor, The (1965), 42
Midsummer Night's Dream, A (1935), 16
Midsummer Night's Dream, A (1959), 17
Midsummer Night's Dream, A (1967), 42
Midsummer Night's Dream, A (1968), 17
Moor's Pavane, The, 42
Much Ado About Nothing (International Film Bureau Series), 48
Much Ado About Nothing (Fair Adventure Series), 49

Ophelia, 26
Othello (1952), 17
Othello (1956), 18
Othello (1965), 18
Othello (Fair Adventure Series), 49
Othello (International Film Bureau Series), 48

Panic Button, 34
Prince of Players, 35
Printing of the Plays, The, 49

Rest Is Silence, The, 25
Richard II (Fair Adventure Series), 49
Richard II (International Film Bureau Series), 48
Richard III (1956), 18

Richard III (Fair Adventure Series), 49
Richard III (International Film Bureau Series), 48
Romanoff and Juliet, 34
Romeo and Juliet (1936), 19
Romeo and Juliet (1944), 33
Romeo and Juliet (1965), 19
Romeo and Juliet (1966), 44
Romeo and Juliet (1964—Italy/Spain), 19
Romeo and Juliet (1968—Great Britain/Italy), 19
Romeo and Juliet (Fair Adventure Series), 49
Romeo and Juliet (International Film Bureau Series), 48
Romeo and Juliet (National Geographic Series), 48

Secret Sex Lives of Romeo and Juliet, The, 35
Shakespeare of Stratford and London, 48
Shakespeare's Stratford, 49
Shakespeare's Theater, 49
Shakespeare's World and Shakespeare's London, 49
Shaw vs. Shakespeare: Caesar and Cleopatra, 50
Shaw vs. Shakespeare: The Character of Caesar, 50
Shaw vs. Shakespeare: The Tragedy of Julius Caesar, 50
Show of Shows, 26
Star Crossed Love, 48
Sweet Light in a Dark Room, 33

Taming of the Shrew, The (1929), 20
Taming of the Shrew, The (1967), 20
Taming of the Shrew, The (International Film Bureau Series), 48
Tempest, The (Fair Adventure Series), 49
Tempest, The (International Film Bureau Series), 48
Test Shots for Hamlet, 53
Time Is Out of Joint, The, 47
Throne of Blood, 29
To Be Or Not Be Be, 25
Tower of London (1939), 32
Tower of London (1962), 32
Twelfth Night (1955), 20
Twelfth Night (Fair Adventure Series), 49

West Side Story, 43
What Happens in Hamlet, 50

About the Author

Barry Parker first became interested in film when his mother took him to see Walt Disney's *20,000 Leagues Under The Sea* in 1954. Sometime after this event, Mr. Parker saw several thousand other films, and divided his time between film viewing and writing. A member of The New York Times Washington Bureau between 1973-1976, his work has appeared in the *Times*, *The Washington Post*, and on National Public Radio's *All Things Considered*, among others. He joined the staff of The Folger Library in October, 1978.